PRETTY PÂTISSERIE

MAKIKO SEARLE

First published in September 2015
by B. Dutton Publishing Limited,
The Grange, Hones Yard, Farnham,
Surrey, GU9 8BB, UK.
Copyright: Makiko Searle 2015

ISBN-13: 978-1-905113-39-2

Publisher: Beverley Dutton

Group Editor: Jennifer Kelly

Art Director/Designer: Sarah Ryan

Book publishing

Copy Editor: Frankie New

Photography: Anna Rosell

Photography on pages 95 and 97 by Rob Goves

Photography on pages 78, 93, 104–107 and 164 by
Makiko Searle

Magazine publishing

Editor: Jenny Royle

Copy Editor: Adele Duthie

Senior Graphic Designer: Zena Deakin

PR and Advertising Manager: Natalie Bull

Props supplied by Classic Crockery Hire,
www.classiccrockery.co.uk

Ceramics supplied by Etsuko Kato,
www.h5.dion.ne.jp/~claywork/

Edible flowers by Maddock's Farm Organics,
www.maddocksfarmorganics.co.uk

Printed by 1010 Printing Ltd., China

Disclaimer

PRETTY PÂTISSERIE

Decorative and delicious ideas for dinner parties, weddings, afternoon tea and other special occasions

ACKNOWLEDGEMENTS

It was just after I wrote my first book, *Cakes to Fall in Love With*, that I was lucky enough to sign up for a second book with B. Dutton Publishing.

On 11th March 2011, there was a huge earthquake in the north of Japan which should still be fresh in everyone's memories. Although, luckily, all my family and close friends were safe, I was emotionally affected by this traumatic disaster for a long time. Without encouragement, I would have given up on this great opportunity by now so I cannot thank everyone enough who encouraged me to complete this project over the past four years, especially to all the team at B. Dutton Publishing for their professional attitude.

I would like to give special thanks to Beverley and Robert Dutton for giving me another opportunity to publish a book. I will never forget your kindness and encouragement in the letter you sent and I feel so honoured to be involved in another book.

I really appreciate Jennifer Kelly and Frankie New for their fantastic editing work, and especially for being patient with me when there were delays and changes to the publication plans.

I'd like to thank Sarah Ryan for her fantastic design skills – your work inspired me to carry on working and to finish when I was almost beginning to give up.

I would also like to send a huge thanks to Anna Rosell for her fabulous and beautiful work, driven by her passion for photography. It is not an exaggeration, without your generous time and effort I could not have achieved such a lovely book.

To the talented Daniela Johnston, thank you very much for your generosity and kindness and for the use of some of your beautiful crockery collection.

Thanks to my lovely staff and friends, Yuki, Angela, Liina and Bunny for all your help and support.

Huge thanks and all my love to my family!

DEDICATION

I would like to dedicate this book to those who have lost their beloved family and friends in natural disasters. I pray their souls may rest in peace.

INTRODUCTION

My background as a pastry chef meant that I have always wanted to write a pâtisserie book, so I was over the moon when I got the chance to publish *Pretty Pâtisserie*. Although I have many years of experience working in pastry kitchens, writing a book for home bakers was harder than I initially imagined. All the recipes I used to create were on a much larger scale and involved using professional equipment, so I have spent time adapting these so you can easily make them at home in your own kitchen.

The term 'pâtisserie' covers a wide range of recipes, but I have narrowed it down to four main chapters which include my all-time favourites: biscuits and cookies, sponge cakes, choux pastry and chocolate treats. Each chapter has a selection of different recipes and provides inspirational ways to decorate them, with something for all levels of ability. I wanted to create a book that not only provides you with delicious recipes, but shows you how to decorate and present them, too.

I have also made sure to include step-by-step pictures throughout the book to help you along the way, as well as top tips for using up leftover ingredients. Remember that you can always adapt the ideas in this book – try experimenting with the decoration, filling or flavour combinations to create your own pâtisserie!

I hope that my selection of pretty pâtisserie will inspire you and that you'll enjoy creating sweet treats to share with friends and family, whether it's a special occasion or you just want to brighten someone's day.

Maki

CONTENTS

12–69

70–107

BISCUITS & COOKIES

SPONGE CAKES

BASIC EDIBLES & EQUIPMENT

Baking paper, parchment paper or silicone paper is a baking staple and will ensure that your cakes, biscuits and pastries won't stick to your bakeware. This is different to greaseproof paper, which is used to wrap cakes and biscuits once they are baked.

book use this method so that you don't need to add a raising agent.

slab will allow the chocolate to set quicker and speed up your work.

Good-quality **baking trays** that don't warp are essential for many techniques including pâte décor and the thin layers required in a gâteau opéra. I use the multi-size square cake pan from Silverwood as you can adjust the size for different projects.

Cake boards and drums are available in different thicknesses, shapes and sizes and are ideal for presenting cakes and desserts.

Many of the recipes in this book have lemon, lime and orange flavour options so a **citrus squeezer** comes in useful.

A metal or plastic **ball tool** is useful for making decorative blossoms – working on a foam pad or in the palm of your hand, push the tool into the centre of the flower to give it a natural cupped shape.

A **balloon whisk** will incorporate air into a mixture and keep it light, such as when mixing meringue into cake batter. Many of the recipes in this

Choose good-quality, heavy-duty **cake tins** that won't warp and promote even heat distribution for best results.

A **chocolate scraper** is an essential piece of equipment for making chocolate decorations. Spreading the chocolate onto a frozen marble

A **citrus zester** is also a handy tool to have.

Cling film is essential for wrapping cakes if you are planning to store or freeze them for a short amount of time. For longer periods, seal cakes in a food bag or airtight container after wrapping as cling film is slightly porous. I also use it to line baking dishes when I am assembling layered desserts.

If you're making any of the cookie or biscuit projects in this book you will need **cookie cutters** in your chosen shapes. They are also useful for cutting shapes from ready-to-roll pastes such as marzipan and sugarpaste (rolled fondant) to decorate cookies or cakes.

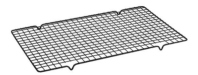

Before decorating, icing or filling your bakes, make sure you allow enough time to allow them to cool completely on a **cooling rack**.

A **cranked palette knife** is used to spread sponge batter, melted chocolate and fillings evenly. It is also ideal for picking up biscuits, decorations and small decorative pieces, minimising the risk of breakages.

If you're baking any of the cupcakes featured in this book, choose co-ordinating **cupcake cases** to

present them in. Those made from thicker paper won't go see-through when baked. You will also need a **cupcake tin** to make them in.

If you're tempering chocolate or making syrup, jam or mousse, a **digital thermometer** will make it easy to ensure you are working to the correct temperatures for best results.

Dust (powder) food colours can be used for surface painting as well as in melted white chocolate, icings, macaroon mix and cake mixes. Check that the colourings you are using are completely edible and suitable for food use (see suppliers on page 206).

Keep a pair of stainless steel **fine scissors** in your decorating

kit as they are always handy for snipping piping bags, opening icing packs, etc.

Use a **fine sieve** to sift all flours and sugars as this will minimise lumps and ensure your bakes have a light texture.

Pure **gold and silver leaf** are entirely edible and add an opulent touch to desserts, pastries, biscuits and cakes. The leaf is exceptionally fine so use the tip of a paintbrush or tweezers to carefully place it.

For best results when making caramel, jams and syrups, use a **heavy-based saucepan**.

Use an **icing sugar shaker** with a fine mesh top to prevent biscuit dough and roll-out pastes from sticking.

A **kitchen timer** will ensure you keep accurate timings when baking.

When cutting sponge cakes into layers, always use a **large, serrated knife** and cut through gently using a sawing action.

A **small, sharp knife** has a multitude of uses so keep one in your baking kit.

Liquid food colours can be used to add colour to cake and pastry

batters, buttercream, icings and jellies. As with all colourings, check that the products you are using are completely edible (see suppliers on page 206).

Make sure you keep all **mixing bowls** clean and free from grease before use and only use heatproof bowls in the microwave.

A **non-stick board** is useful for rolling out pastes for decoration. Placing a piece of non-slip mat underneath will hold it in place as you work.

Keep a selection of **paintbrushes** in your decorating kit, from fine tips for surface painting details to wide brushes for applying dust colours.

You will need a **pastry brush** for brushing sugar syrup onto sponges

and for glazing pastries. Silicone is best as it won't lose its bristles.

Disposable **piping bags** are essential for any pastry chef. Use large, plastic bags for piping batter and fillings and smaller, paper bags for adding decorative piping in royal icing or chocolate. You can also use squeezy bottles for flooding run-outs or piping chocolate if you prefer.

Piping nozzles (tips) can be used in both plastic and paper piping bags to create a wide variety of different patterns and borders as well as petals and leaves. Savoy (large) nozzles are for use with large bags and small, metal nozzles with greaseproof paper bags.

A **large, heavy rolling pin** will make easy work of rolling out biscuit dough, marzipan and cake coverings.

A **small rolling pin** is used with roll-out pastes such as flower paste, sugarpaste (rolled fondant), marzipan and modelling chocolate to make small decorations.

Keep a **ruler** solely for baking use and wash it regularly.

Reliable, accurate **scales** are the secret to successful baking and pâtisserie. Use either metric or imperial weights and measures rather than a combination of both.

A **scriber** (or scribing tool) is useful for marking out guidelines or patterns onto cakes and bakes, particularly if you need to cut neat, equal portions.

There is a huge range of **silicone bakeware** on the market which means you can make individual desserts that look professional. Smaller silicone moulds can also be used to make chocolates, or you may prefer the more traditional polycarbonate chocolate moulds which are made from rigid plastic.

Choose a flexible, **silicone spatula** for use with cake and pastry batters and melted chocolate.

Spacers are incredibly useful for rolling out biscuit dough and ready-to-roll icings and coverings evenly. Place either side of the dough/paste before rolling out.

A **stand mixer** will save you time and effort when baking.

When adding detailed decoration, particularly when piping on the sides of a cake, I recommend using a **turntable** so it is easy to turn the cake. One on a stand will also elevate your work so is useful for decorating cookies.

TOP TIP

Where the weight of eggs is important for the success of a recipe, I have given the amount in grams and ounces. The approximate number of eggs needed is also given as a guide, however, I would recommend weighing the eggs so that you can measure them accurately. As a general rule, a medium-sized egg out of the shell weighs approximately 50g (1³/₄oz) of which ²/₃ is egg white (approximately 35g/1¹/₄oz) and ¹/₃ is yolk (approximately 15g/¹/₂oz).

The basic vanilla biscuit recipe at the beginning of this chapter makes quite firm biscuits which are ideal for decorating. Almost all of the projects in this book use this recipe, but you'll also find a chocolate cookie recipe and a maple syrup biscuit recipe with decorative ideas at the end of this chapter.

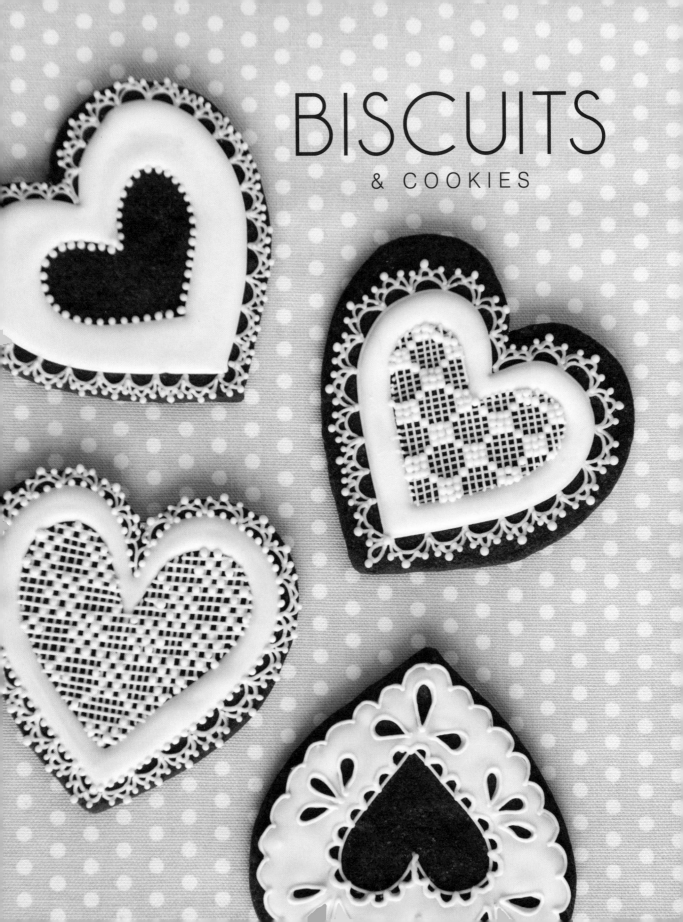

BISCUITS

& COOKIES

BASIC VANILLA BISCUITS

INGREDIENTS

125g (4½oz) unsalted butter, softened
125g (4½oz) caster sugar
32g (1oz) egg (approximately ½ large egg)
1 vanilla pod
250g (8¾oz) plain flour

EQUIPMENT

Basic equipment (see pages 8–11)

MAKES APPROXIMATELY 15 LARGE OR 30 SMALL BISCUITS

1 Preheat the oven to 180°C/350°F/gas mark 4.

2 Cream the butter and caster sugar together until pale in colour. Add the egg and mix in well, then stir in the seeds from the vanilla pod.

3 Add the flour little by little until it is all combined: take care not to overmix the flour.

4 Form the dough into a flat square shape with your hands, wrap it in cling film and allow to rest in the fridge for one hour.

5 Take the dough out of the fridge and flatten it with your palm. Lightly dust the work surface with flour to prevent the dough from sticking, but use sparingly otherwise the dough may become too dry. Roll out the dough with a large rolling pin and, when it's almost flat, place a piece of baking paper underneath it.

6 Place 5mm (¼") spacers either side and continue to roll out until the dough is flat and even. A 5mm (¼") thickness is ideal for large biscuits, but continue to roll out to 4mm (³/₁₆") for small or medium biscuits. Chill the sheet of biscuit dough in the fridge for one hour until firm.

7 Remove the dough from the fridge and cut out as many shapes as you can with a cookie cutter. Knead the dough trimmings together, roll it out again and cut out as many shapes as you can. (Remember that the more you knead the dough, the tougher it will become.) If the shapes are firm enough to lift, place them onto a baking tray lined with baking paper and leave space between them to allow for spreading. If they are too soft, put them in the fridge until they firm up.

8 Bake for 10–15 minutes or until golden brown; the biscuits may need a little longer depending on their size. Allow to cool completely before decorating.

9 Store in an airtight container for up to two weeks.

FLAVOUR VARIATIONS

LEMON: add the finely grated zest of one lemon after mixing in the egg.

ORANGE: add the finely grated zest from ²/₃ of an orange after mixing in the egg.

CHOCOLATE: replace ¼ of the plain flour with cocoa powder.

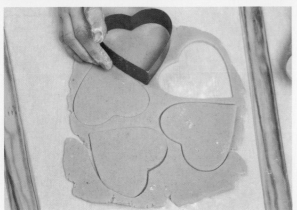

TOP TIP

If you want to make the biscuits using a template, draw the desired shape onto a piece of food-grade card (e.g. from a cake box) or acetate and cut it out. Place the template on a sheet of biscuit dough and cut around it with a small, sharp knife. Acetate templates can always be wiped clean and used again.

ROYAL ICING

INGREDIENTS

15g (½oz) pasteurized, dried albumen powder*
75ml (2½fl oz) pre-boiled, lukewarm water
500g (1lb 1¾oz) icing sugar

1 Mix the powdered albumen and pre-boiled, lukewarm water in a bowl until the powder has completely dissolved.

2 Sift the icing sugar into a mixing bowl. Pass the liquid albumen through a sieve and add it to the sugar.

3 Using the paddle attachment, mix in a stand mixer at a low speed for approximately five minutes until light and fluffy. The correct consistency has been reached when the icing is whiter and will stand up in firm peaks (stiff-peak consistency, see opposite).

4 Transfer the icing to a large plastic piping bag or a clean bowl with a clean, damp tea towel on top to stop a crust forming on the icing. If you don't need to use the icing straight away, place it in a plastic container with a piece of cling film over the top. Make sure the top of the container is completely covered. Place the lid on securely and store at room temperature until required.

*Follow the instructions for use on the back of the packet of albumen powder you are using as the strength of albumen can differ depending on the product.

CONSISTENCIES OF ROYAL ICING

STIFF PEAK

This consistency is suitable for piping leaves, flowers and for use between stacked cakes to hold them in place. When lifted with a palette knife the icing should form stiff peaks that do not bend over.

If you are piping with stiff-peak icing, you will need to remove some of the air from the icing first. Using a palette knife, take some icing out of the bowl and rub/paddle it back and forth on a clean surface before placing it into a piping bag.

SOFT PEAK

This consistency is suitable for pressure piping and stencilling onto the sides of cakes and for the outline of run-out decorations on cookies. Add a few drops of pre-boiled, cold water at a time to stiff-peak icing, lifting the icing with a palette knife after each addition. The icing should form soft peaks that bend over at the tip. Using a palette knife, take some icing out of the bowl and rub it back and forth on a clean surface until it is smooth before placing it into a piping bag.

DOT

This consistency is ideal for piping round dots as part of a cake or cookie design. To achieve this consistency, add a few drops of pre-boiled water at a time to soft-peak consistency icing, lifting the icing with a palette knife after each addition. The icing should form peaks but these will disappear back into the bowl after a few seconds. Dot consistency should be runnier than soft-peak consistency, but not as fluid as run-out consistency (see below).

RUN-OUT

This consistency is suitable for flooding in run-outs, including when decorating cookies and biscuits. Place some icing in a bowl, add a few drops of pre-boiled, cold water and stir. Cut through the icing with a palette knife: the consistency is correct if it flows back together after 10 seconds. If it takes longer, gradually add a little more water. To flood inside a piped outline, place the run-out icing into either a paper piping bag with the tip cut off, or a squeezy bottle, whichever you prefer.

STIFF PEAK

SOFT PEAK

RUN-OUT

BUTTERFLY BISCUITS

EDIBLES

1 x vanilla biscuit recipe (see page 14)
1 x royal icing recipe (see page 16)
Paste food colours: ivory, pale yellow, pink

EQUIPMENT

Basic equipment (see pages 8–11)
Small butterfly cookie cutter
7 small bowls
Piping nozzles: nos. 1.5, 3 x 2

MAKES 30–35 SMALL BUTTERFLY BISCUITS

1 Roll out the biscuit dough to 4mm (³/₁₆") thick and cut out 30–35 butterfly shapes with the cookie cutter. Bake the biscuits for 10–15 minutes, as per the recipe on page 14. Leave on a wire rack to cool.

2 Make up a batch of stiff-peak royal icing (see page 17) and put approximately 100g (3½oz) of the icing to one side. Divide the remaining icing into three different bowls and colour each with a different paste food colour: pink, yellow and a mixture of pink and yellow to make peach. You will only need to colour the icing with a touch of paste colour to achieve a light, pastel shade.

3 Place 2–3tbsp of each colour icing in separate bowls, then add a few drops of pre-boiled, cold water to each

one to make soft-peak consistency (see page 17). Fit three paper piping bags with no. 2 nozzles and fill with the pink, yellow and peach icing respectively. Pipe around the outline of each butterfly biscuit with soft-peak royal icing.

4 Add a little more pre-boiled, cold water to each colour of the remaining icing to achieve run-out consistency (see page 17). Prepare another piping bag or an icing squeezy bottle with each colour of runny icing. Flood inside the alternate sections of the outline of each biscuit with the run-out icing. Leave for at least four to five hours until the surface is completely dry.

5 Once dry, colour the 100g (3½oz) of icing you put aside earlier with a touch of ivory paste food colour and add a few drops of pre-boiled water to make it soft-peak consistency. Fit a paper piping bag with a no. 1.5 nozzle and fill with the ivory-coloured icing. Pipe around the outline of the butterfly wings first, then use the picture opposite as a guide to pipe the detail on the wings.

6 To finish, use the ivory icing to pipe a line between the wings for the body then a bulb above it for the head and leave to dry.

TOP TIPS

Make sure to cover any royal icing that you are not using with a damp tea towel to stop it crusting over.

If you don't have the correct piping nozzles, you can always snip off the tip of the paper piping bag to the size you need.

EASTER EGG BISCUITS

EDIBLES

1 x vanilla biscuit recipe (see page 14)
1 x royal icing recipe (see page 16)
Paste food colours: blue, green, pink, yellow

EQUIPMENT

Basic equipment (see pages 8–11)
Easter egg cookie cutter
4 small bowls
Cotton thread or ribbon

MAKES 80–85 SMALL, 40–45 MEDIUM, OR 25–30 LARGE EASTER EGG BISCUITS

1 Roll out the biscuit dough to 5mm (¼") thick and cut out 30 large egg shapes with the cutter. Bake the biscuits for 10–15 minutes, as per the recipe on page 14. Leave on a wire rack to cool.

2 Make up some soft-peak royal icing (see page 17), divide the icing into four bowls and colour each bowlful with a different paste colour.

3 Place 2–3tbsp of each colour icing into separate paper piping bags, then snip the tip off the end of each bag. Pipe around the outline of each biscuit with soft-peak icing in the colour of your choice.

4 Add a few drops of cold, pre-boiled water to the remaining icing until you achieve a run-out consistency (see page 17). Fill four more paper piping bags or icing squeezy bottles with the different colours of run-out icing and snip off the tips of the bags. Flood inside the outline around the biscuit with run-out icing of the same colour.

5 As soon as you have flooded the cookie, pipe small dots or stripes on the icing with soft-peak icing in the colour of your choice. To make a wavy pattern, pipe lines across the cookie in a contrasting colour and pull a cocktail stick through the lines so that the colour runs.

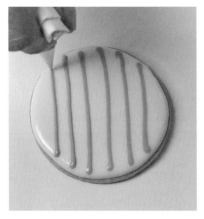

6 Leave the cookies until the surface of the icing is nearly dry then use a scribing tool to make a small hole at the top of the egg. Make sure you do this before the icing has dried or you may crack the surface of the icing. Leave them to dry completely, then insert a cotton thread through the hole and tie it so that you can hang the biscuit as a decoration.

TOP TIP

If you prefer to use a decorative ribbon to hang the biscuits, it is better to make a slightly larger hole in the dough before you bake them. Remember to decorate around the hole as you are icing the biscuits.

If you are confident at piping, you could create the basic Easter egg biscuits following the steps above then embellish them with the cross-stitch effect explained on page 68. These ornate biscuits would make great Easter gifts for adults or are perfect as afternoon tea treats.

FLORAL WREATH BISCUITS

EDIBLES

1 x vanilla biscuit recipe (see page 14)

1 x royal icing recipe (see page 16)

Paste food colours: blue, green, pink, purple, yellow

EQUIPMENT

Basic equipment (see pages 8–11)

Round cutters: 7cm and 3cm (2¾" and 1⅛")

Narrow satin ribbon in a colour of your choice

MAKES 15 SMALL WREATH BISCUITS

1 Prepare all the piped flowers in advance. Make up some royal icing to stiff-peak consistency (see page 17) and divide it between five bowls. Use the paste food colours to make the icing dark blue, light blue, pale pink, purple and pale yellow respectively. Following the instructions on page 188, pipe 45–60 dark blue pansies, pale pink pansies, purple four-petal flowers, light blue five-petal flowers and light yellow roses. Pipe the flowers using a no. 57 nozzle to make them slightly smaller. Leave to dry overnight.

2 Roll out the biscuit dough to 4mm (³⁄₁₆") thick and cut out 10 circles with a 7cm (2¾") round cutter. Cut out the

centre of each biscuit with a 3cm (1⅛") round cutter to make a ring. Bake for 10–15 minutes, as per the recipe on page 14. Leave on a wire rack to cool.

3 Make up some firm-peak and soft-peak royal icing (see page 17), prepare a paper piping bag of each and snip off the very tip of the bags. Colour the rest of the firm-peak icing with green and a touch of yellow paste food colours, then prepare a third piping bag with this pale green royal icing.

4 Use the firm-peak white icing to attach the ready-made piped flowers neatly around each ring, following the picture as a guide.

5 Pipe small five-petal flowers (see page 192) with the soft-peak white icing and small leaves (see page 192) with the pale green icing to fill any gaps between the flowers.

6 Once the icing is dry, loop a thin satin ribbon through the ring and tie it in a bow so you can hang the wreath as a decoration.

TOP TIP

If the dough is too soft to lift, put it back in the fridge and leave to firm up before trying to move the biscuit shapes onto the tray.

SEASONAL WREATHS

You can adapt the floral wreath biscuits easily to make more seasonal designs. For an Easter wreath, colour some firm-peak royal icing light green and pipe rows of leaves (see page 192) around the biscuit using a leaf nozzle (or simply cut a V-shape into the end of a paper piping bag). Once dry, pipe white five-petal flowers around the wreath to finish the design (see page 192).

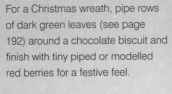

For a Christmas wreath, pipe rows of dark green leaves (see page 192) around a chocolate biscuit and finish with tiny piped or modelled red berries for a festive feel.

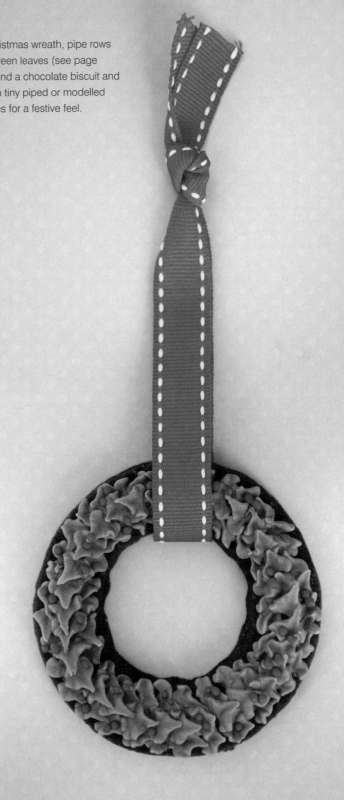

ROSE BISCUITS

EDIBLES

1 x vanilla biscuit recipe (see page 14)
1 x royal icing recipe (see page 16)
Paste food colours: ivory, pale blue

EQUIPMENT

Basic equipment (see pages 8–11)
6cm (2³/₈") round cutter
Piping nozzles: nos. 1, 1.5

MAKES 30 ROUND BISCUITS

1 Roll out the biscuit dough to 4mm (³/₁₆") thick and cut out 30–35 circles with a 6cm (2³/₈") round cutter. Bake the biscuits for 10–15 minutes, as per the recipe on page 14. Leave on a wire rack to cool.

2 Make up a batch of royal icing to soft-peak consistency (see page 17) and divide the icing between two bowls. Colour one bowl of icing with a touch of pale blue paste food colour and the second bowl with a touch of ivory.

3 Fill a paper piping bag ²/₃ full with the pale blue soft-peak icing then snip off the very end of the bag. Pipe a circle outline centrally on the biscuit approximately 7mm (¼") from the edge.

TOP TIP

If you aren't confident piping circles freehand, you could always make a circle template from greaseproof paper and place it in the centre of each biscuit as you pipe.

4 Add a few drops of cold, pre-boiled water to the remaining blue icing to make it a run-out consistency (see page 17). Flood inside the circle with the pale blue runny icing and leave to dry completely.

5 Place some ivory-coloured icing in a paper piping bag fitted with a no. 1.5 nozzle. Working outwards from

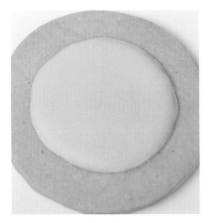
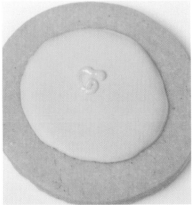

the centre of the blue circle, pipe the rose design following the step pictures as a guide. After you pipe the first petal, dampen a small paintbrush and place it on the edge of the petal. Stroke the icing in towards the centre of the flower. Repeat with each petal until the rose is fully formed.

TOP TIP

Only dampen the paintbrush slightly otherwise it will be too wet to use.

6 Fit a paper piping bag with a no. 1 nozzle and fill ⅔ with some more ivory-coloured soft-peak icing. Pipe a small dot at the edge of the blue circle, then pipe another dot directly opposite the first on the other side of the circle. Pipe a third dot halfway between the first two dots, then pipe another directly opposite the third dot. You should have four dots equally spaced around the blue circle.

7 In between each of these dots, pipe three more dots so you have 16 dots equally spaced around the circle. Pipe an arch from one dot to the next. Once you have joined up all the dots, pipe three smaller arches on the curve of each of the larger arches.

8 To finish, pipe dots of icing above each small arch as shown in the picture, and leave to dry.

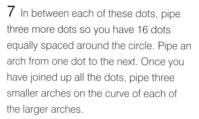

TOP TIP

For a simpler border, pipe the outline for the run-out closer to the edge then add a row of dots around the outside.

GOLD LEAF
BISCUIT
WREATH

GOLD LEAF BISCUIT WREATH

EDIBLES

1 x vanilla biscuit recipe (see page 14)
8–10 sheets of edible gold leaf (SK)
½ x royal icing recipe (see page 16)
Paste food colour: brown
Small amount of flour

EQUIPMENT

Basic equipment (see pages 8–11)
SK Cut & Form Mould: Oak Leaf
Wide satin ribbon in a colour of your choice

MAKES 16 LEAF BISCUITS FOR ONE WREATH

1 Sprinkle a small amount of flour inside the bottom half of the oak leaf mould then fill with biscuit dough. Push down on the dough to impress the veins and trim away any excess with a small, sharp knife. Bend back the mould slightly to release the dough and gently turn out the leaf shape. Repeat to make another 15 leaf-shaped biscuits.

2 Bake for 13–15 minutes, following the recipe on page 14. Leave on a wire rack to cool.

3 Take a sheet of gold leaf on its backing paper with a covering sheet on top and cut it in half so it is roughly the same size as the biscuit. Peel back one of the thin paper sheets, then place a biscuit face-down onto it and gently push down. Turn the biscuit over and gently tap the paper with your fingers until the gold leaf is stuck down. Peel back the other piece of paper and if any gold leaf comes unstuck, gently brush it back down with a dry, soft brush. Repeat for each of the leaf biscuits.

4 Draw a 20cm (7¾") diameter circle on a piece of paper to make a template for the wreath. Place a piece of greaseproof paper over the template and arrange the leaf biscuits face-down around the circle. Make sure that the biscuits overlap each other slightly.

5 Once you have arranged all the biscuits, make up some stiff-peak royal icing (see page 17) and colour it with brown paste food colour. Use the icing to stick the leaves to each other.

6 Leave the completed wreath to dry overnight and allow all the leaves to set in place. To add a decorative finish, tie a large satin bow around the top of the wreath and leave the tails to hang down.

TOP TIP

If you prefer, you could add a small amount of coffee extract to the royal icing instead to achieve a similar colour.

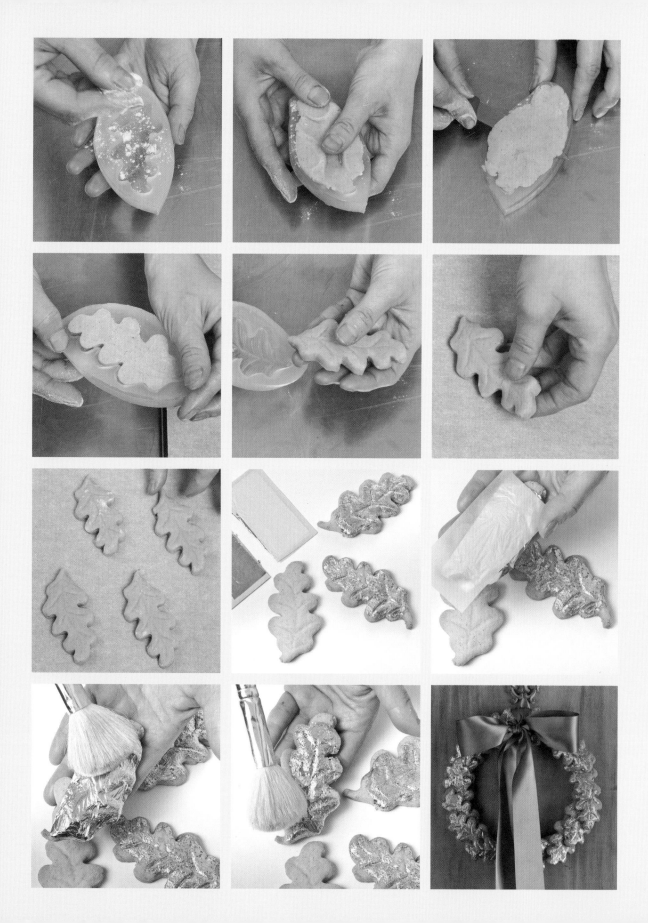

SNOWFLAKE BISCUITS

EDIBLES

1 x vanilla biscuit recipe (see page 14)

1 x royal icing recipe (see page 16)

Small amount of caster sugar

Edible White Magic Sparkles, crushed

EQUIPMENT

Basic equipment (see pages 8–11)

Large and small snowflake cookie cutters

Large snowflake cookie cutter (different design)

Small diamond-shaped cutter

Piping nozzles: nos. 1.5, 2

MAKES 15 SNOWFLAKE BISCUITS (FIVE OF EACH DESIGN)

1 Roll out the biscuit dough to 4mm (³/₁₆") thick. For Design 1, cut out five snowflake shapes with the large snowflake cutter, then use the small snowflake cutter to cut out the centre of each biscuit. For Design 2, cut out another five large snowflakes, then use a small diamond cutter to cut out 12 diamonds from around each of the larger snowflakes. For Design 3, cut out five more biscuits with the large snowflake cutter of a different design. Bake for 10–15 minutes, following the recipe on page 14. Leave on a wire rack to cool completely.

DESIGN 1

2 Make up some soft-peak royal icing (see page 17), fit a paper piping bag with a no. 2 piping nozzle and fill ²/₃ with the icing. Prepare some run-out consistency royal icing and place it in another paper piping bag, or an icing squeezy bottle if you prefer.

3 Use the soft-peak icing to pipe an outline around the edges of the snowflake. Snip off the tip of the other piping

DESIGN 1

DESIGN 2

DESIGN 3

bag or use the squeezy bottle and flood inside the outline with white run-out icing.

4 Before the icing dries, sprinkle with caster sugar and crushed Magic Sparkles to add shimmer. Leave the icing to dry then brush away any excess with a dry, soft brush.

DESIGN 2

5 Fit a paper piping bag with a no. 2 nozzle and fill with some soft-peak icing. Pipe straight lines around the outline of the biscuit to create the shape of a snowflake. Sprinkle with caster sugar and crushed Magic Sparkles while the icing is still wet.

6 Pipe a small dot of royal icing in the centre and at each point of the snowflake and leave to dry completely.

DESIGN 3

7 Fit a paper piping bag with a no. 1.5 nozzle and fill with some soft-peak royal icing. Pipe a hexagon with curved sides in the centre of the biscuit, as shown in the picture.

8 Pipe a straight line from one corner of the hexagon to the opposite corner, then join up the other corners in the same way. Pipe a bulb of icing in the centre where the lines cross over each other.

9 Pipe a six-point star inside the hexagon so that each point of the star sits in the middle of each side of the hexagon. Pipe a V-shape at each corner of the hexagon between the dots and the star shape.

10 From the middle of one side of the hexagon, pipe a straight line out along one point of the snowflake, then pipe two swirls coming out from either side of the first line. Repeat for all the points of the snowflake.

11 Sprinkle with caster sugar and crushed Magic Sparkles while the icing is still wet and leave to dry completely.

BRODERIE ANGLAISE BISCUITS

EDIBLES

1 x vanilla biscuit recipe (see page 14)
1 x royal icing recipe (see page 16)
Paste food colour: ivory (optional)

EQUIPMENT

Basic equipment (see pages 8–11)
Piping nozzles: nos. 1, 1.5

MAKES 20–35 RECTANGULAR COOKIES

1 Roll out the biscuit dough into a thin sheet, place on a piece of greaseproof paper and leave it to firm in the fridge.

2 Once firm enough to handle, remove the sheet of dough from the fridge. Use a small, sharp knife and a clean ruler to cut one side of the sheet straight. From this straight edge, measure 3–4cm (1⅛–1½") across and cut another straight line to make a long strip of dough. Keep going in the same way across the dough until you have cut the whole sheet into long strips. Discard any excess dough left on either side of the sheet.

3 Turn the sheet of dough around so that the longer side is facing you. Measure and cut each of the long strips into 8–10cm (3⅛–4") rectangles.

4 Bake for 10–15 minutes, as per the recipe on page 14. Once baked, leave on a wire rack to cool.

TOP TIP

If the dough has become too soft to lift, leave the biscuits on the greaseproof paper and put them back in the fridge to firm up.

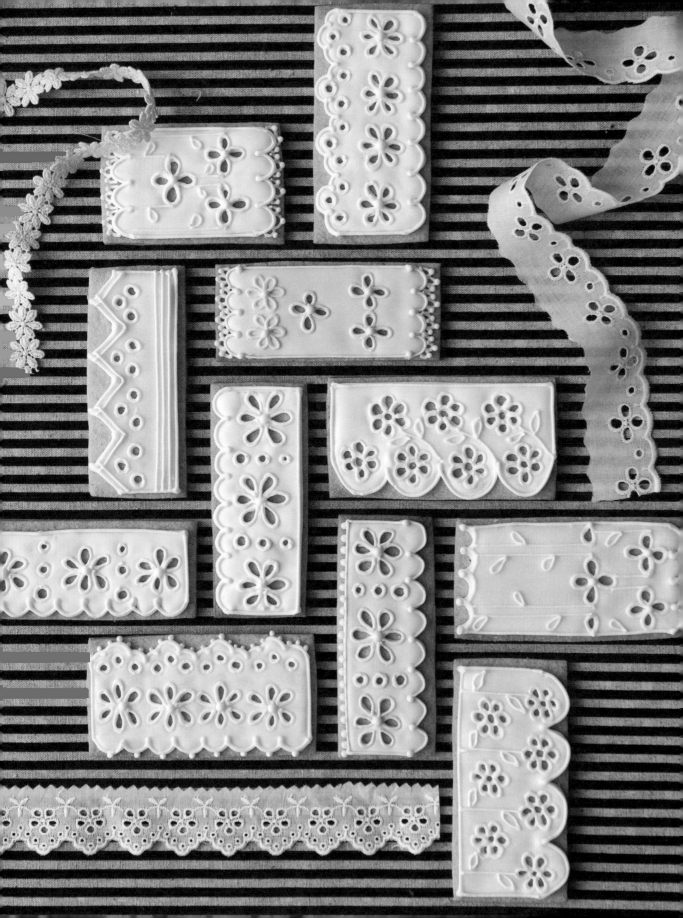

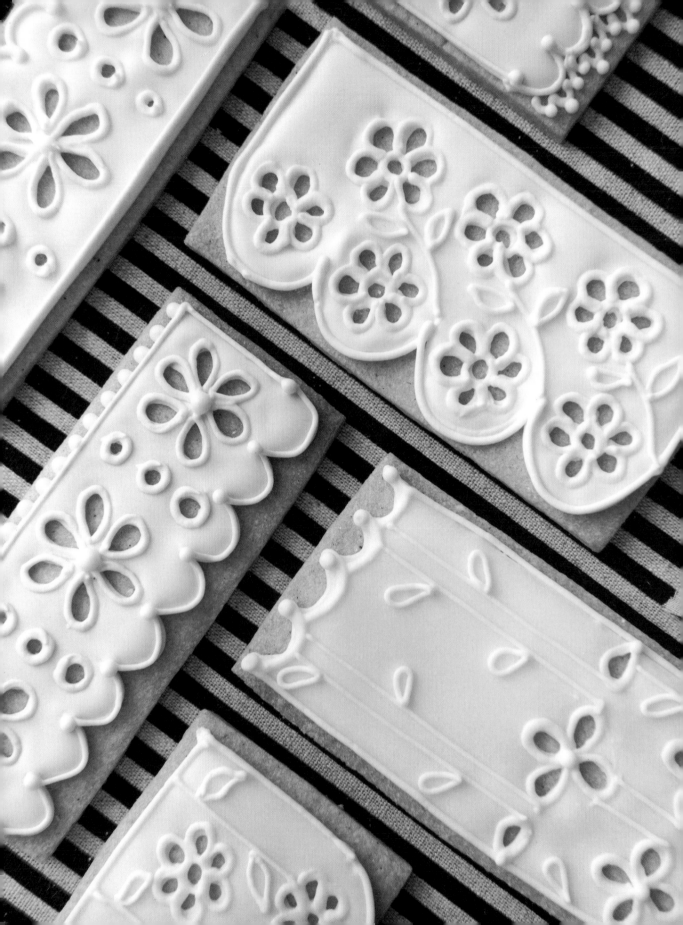

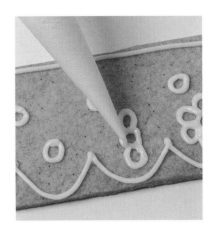

5 Make up some soft-peak royal icing (see page 17) and colour half with a touch of ivory paste food colour, leaving the other half white. I have chosen to decorate some of the biscuits with white icing and some with ivory, but you can leave the icing white if you prefer. Fit a piping bag with a no. 1.5 nozzle and fill ²/₃ with either white or ivory icing.

6 Put aside a small amount of the soft-peak royal icing, then add a few drops of water to the remaining icing to make a run-out consistency (see page 17). Divide the remaining icing between a few paper piping bags then snip off the very tips, or fill an icing squeezy bottle if you prefer.

7 Use the soft-peak icing to pipe a straight line around three sides of the biscuit. To pipe a straight line, make small dots where you want the line to start and finish, then pipe a line from one dot to the other.

8 To make the wavy edge, pipe three equally spaced dots along the fourth side of the biscuit. Join the dots with scallops to create the wave shape, making sure to join up the scallops with the straight outline.

9 For the flower centres, pipe a small circle in each scallop. Pipe three more circles above these to form the second row. Pipe six small circles around each flower centre to make the petals.

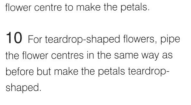

10 For teardrop-shaped flowers, pipe the flower centres in the same way as before but make the petals teardrop-shaped.

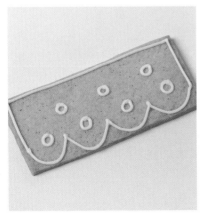

11 Flood inside the outline with run-out icing in your chosen colour, making sure to avoid filling in the flower pattern. Use a cocktail stick or a scribing tool to draw the icing up to the edges of the pattern. Leave for at least four hours to allow the surface of each biscuit to dry completely.

12 Once dry, fit a piping bag with a no. 1 nozzle and fill with the soft-peak icing you put aside earlier. Pipe over the outline and flower decoration to make them more defined and pipe stems and leaves for the top three flowers.

You can adapt this method to create your own variation of the broderie anglaise pattern, using the designs shown here for inspiration.

MINI WEDDING CAKE BISCUITS

EDIBLES

1 x vanilla biscuit recipe (see page 14)

²⁄₃ x royal icing recipe (see page 16)

Liquid food colour: rose pink

A sheet of rice paper

Dust food colour: rose pink

EQUIPMENT

Basic equipment (see pages 8–11)

Round cutters: 3cm, 5cm, 7cm
(1¹⁄₈", 2", 2¾")

Piping nozzle: no. 1.5

Cherry blossom craft punch

MAKES THREE MINI WEDDING CAKE BISCUITS

1 Roll out the biscuit dough to 4mm (³⁄₁₆") thick and cut out nine round biscuits with each of the three different-sized cutters. Line three baking trays and place biscuits of the same size onto each tray. Bake the 3cm (1¹⁄₈") and 5cm (2") biscuits for approximately 10 minutes. The larger 7cm (2¾") biscuits will need approximately 15 minutes. Leave to cool on a wire rack.

2 Make up some royal icing to soft-peak consistency (see page 17) and colour pale pink with a touch of rose pink liquid food colour. Fill a paper piping bag ²⁄₃ full with the icing and snip off the very tip of the bag. Add some pre-

boiled, cold water to the remaining icing to make a run-out consistency (see page 17) and place this in another paper piping bag, or an icing squeezy bottle if you prefer.

3 Pipe an outline around each of the round biscuits with soft-peak icing, then fill in the centre with run-out icing. Allow the surface to dry completely.

4 Stack three 7cm (2¾") cookies on top of each other, using a small amount of royal icing to stick them together. Stack the 5cm (2") and 3cm (1¹⁄₈") diameter cookies on top to create a tiered wedding cake shape. Leave to set.

If you are a little more confident at piping, you could use soft-peak icing and a no. 1.5 nozzle to pipe sets of scallops around each biscuit tier.

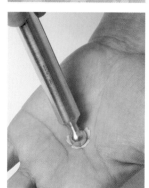

5 Make the icing slightly softer than soft-peak icing to dot consistency (see page 17). Fit a piping bag with a no. 1.5 nozzle and fill with the softer icing. Pipe evenly spaced dots around the edge of each biscuit.

6 Use a craft punch to cut out several cherry blossoms from the sheet of rice paper and dust them lightly with pink dust food colour. Place each blossom in the palm of your hand and push a ball tool or the tip of your finger into the centre of each flower to cup them slightly.

7 Attach the flowers randomly over the side of the biscuits with a little royal icing.

For a chocolaty alternative, decorate some tempered white chocolate with the transfer sheet of your choice (see page 163). Cut out three chocolate discs of different sizes and stack between the biscuit tiers. Attach some rice paper butterflies to finish.

You can decorate the biscuits to match any wedding colour scheme. Gilding the piping with edible gold paint adds an opulent touch.

DRESSING TABLE BISCUITS

EDIBLES

1 x vanilla biscuit recipe (see page 14)

1 x royal icing recipe (see page 16)

Paste food colours: black, brown, emerald, ivory, lilac, pink, yellow

Lustre dust food colours: Antique Gold, Silver (SK)

2–3 sheets of edible silver leaf (SK)

Clear alcohol, e.g. gin or vodka

EQUIPMENT

Basic equipment (see pages 8–11)

Templates (see pages 196–197)

MAKES 21 DRESSING TABLE BISCUITS (THREE OF EACH DESIGN)

1 Trace the templates onto a piece of greaseproof paper or acetate. Roll out the biscuit dough to 4mm (³/₁₆") thick and cut out three of each design using the templates and a sharp knife (see page 15). Bake the lipstick, compact and powder biscuits for 10–15 minutes, as per the recipe on page 14. Bake the high-heeled shoe and small perfume bottle for 15–20 minutes and the handbag and large perfume bottle for 20–25 minutes. Leave on a wire rack to cool completely.

MAKE-UP COMPACT

2 Make up some soft-peak royal icing (see page 17) and colour a portion with yellow and brown paste food colours to make a golden-brown colour. Fill a paper piping bag ²/₃ full with the soft-peak icing then add a few drops of pre-boiled, cold water to the remaining golden-brown icing to make a run-out consistency (see page 17). Fill a paper piping bag with the run-out icing, or use an icing squeezy bottle if you prefer.

3 Use the soft-peak royal icing to pipe an outline around the edge of each round biscuit. Flood inside the piped circle with the run-out consistency icing and leave to dry completely.

4 Place some white soft-peak royal icing and white run-out consistency icing into paper piping bags and snip off the tips. Pipe the outline of a small circle in the middle of the biscuit with soft-peak white icing, then flood it with white run-out icing. Leave to dry completely.

5 Make up some icing that is slightly softer than soft-peak and colour it with yellow and a touch of brown paste food colours to achieve a similar colour to the first batch of icing. Place into a paper piping bag and pipe eight equally spaced dots around the edge of the larger gold circle. Pipe eight dots around the edge of the small white circle between the ones on the outer edge. Pipe pairs of swirly lines to make heart shapes, using the dots as a guide and applying more pressure on the curve of each line. Pipe two teardrops at the base of each heart. Leave to dry.

6 Mix some Silver lustre dust with clear alcohol and paint over the small white circle. Mix some Antique Gold lustre dust with clear alcohol and paint over the golden-brown parts to finish.

PERFUME BOTTLE WITH TASSEL

7 Colour a portion of soft-peak icing with yellow and brown paste food colours and another with a touch of lilac. Add a few drops of pre-boiled, cold water to the golden-brown and lilac icing to make a run-out consistency (see page 17). Prepare four paper piping bags with the different icings.

8 Snip the tip off the bag of lilac soft-peak icing and pipe the outline of the perfume bottle. Pipe a horizontal line across the widest part of the bottle, then pipe a line down the centre to make a cross. Divide either side of the vertical line into four sections and pipe lines down to the base following the curve of the bottle. Pipe smaller lines from the top of the bottle to the horizontal line.

9 Use the golden-brown soft-peak icing to pipe the outline of the lid and the small oval at the base of the bottle.

10 Flood alternate sections of the perfume bottle with the lilac-coloured run-out icing. When the first sections are dry, flood the remaining sections with the same icing. Flood the lid and the oval at the base of the bottle with golden-brown run-out icing, then leave the biscuit to dry completely.

11 Make up some icing that is slightly softer than soft-peak (see page 17) and colour half of it lilac and half golden-brown. Fit two piping bags with no. 1.5 nozzles and fill each with lilac and golden-brown icing

respectively. Use the corresponding colours to pipe over the outline of the design to make it more defined.

12 Use the golden-brown softer icing to pipe the detail on the bottle lid and the tassel. Leave to dry.

13 Mix Antique Gold lustre dust with some clear alcohol and paint over the golden-brown parts of the bottle.

LIPSTICK

14 Colour a portion of soft-peak royal icing with a touch of yellow and brown food colours, another with a touch of pink food colour and another with emerald food colour. Add a few drops of pre-boiled, cold water to each colour icing to make a run-out consistency (see page 17). Prepare six paper piping bags with the different icings.

15 Use the pink soft-peak icing to pipe the outline of the lipstick, the golden-brown soft-peak icing to pipe the top of the holder and the green soft-peak icing to pipe the base. Use the corresponding run-out colours to flood each section alternately. Leave them to dry.

16 Make up some icing that is slightly softer than soft-peak consistency (see page 17) and colour it pale pink and golden-brown. Use the corresponding colours to pipe over the outline of the design to make it more defined (use golden-brown to pipe over the green parts). Leave to dry.

17 Paint over the golden-brown parts with some Antique Gold lustre dust mixed with clear alcohol.

HIGH-HEELED SHOE

18 Take a portion of white soft-peak icing, colour it with a touch of ivory paste food colour then add a few drops of pre-boiled, cold water to make a run-out consistency (see page 17). Colour some more run-out icing with a touch of yellow and brown paste paste food colours to make beige. Prepare three paper piping bags with the different icings.

19 Pipe around the outline of the shoe with ivory soft-peak icing, leaving a space at the top of the shoe for the foot. Flood inside the outline with ivory run-out icing and flood inside the foot area with beige run-out icing. Leave to dry.

20 Make up some icing that is slightly softer than soft peak (see page 17) and place in a piping bag. Pipe the swirl design over the shoe and finish with a few five-petal flowers (see page 192).

PERFUME BOTTLE WITH ATOMIZER

21 Divide some soft-peak icing into four portions and colour with a touch of pink food colour, a touch of ivory, a touch of black (to make grey) and black respectively. Add a few drops of pre-boiled, cold water to each colour icing

to make a run-out consistency (see page 17). Prepare eight bags with the different icings.

22 Pipe the outline of the perfume bottle slightly to the left of the biscuit to leave space for the atomizer. Use pale pink soft-peak icing for the glass bottle, black soft-peak icing for the bow, grey soft-peak icing for the stopper and ivory soft-peak icing for the atomizer and label. Use the corresponding run-out colours to flood each section alternately. Leave to dry.

23 Use soft-peak ivory icing to pipe the swirly design around the label on the bottle, then pipe your chosen initial in the centre. Use the same icing to pipe vertical lines down the atomizer. Use soft-peak grey icing to pipe the detail on the stopper.

24 Cut a slightly larger hole in the end of the bag of pink soft-peak icing and pipe the tube between the atomizer and the stopper. Leave to dry.

25 Paint the stopper section with a mixture of Silver lustre dust and clear alcohol.

FACE POWDER

26 Colour a portion of soft-peak icing with a touch of yellow and brown food colours. Add a few drops of pre-boiled, cold water to some of the golden-brown icing to make a run-out consistency (see page 17). Prepare two paper piping bags with the different icings.

27 Pipe the outline of the powder box with golden-brown soft-peak icing, then flood with the run-out icing. Leave to dry.

28 Prepare some dot consistency icing (see page 17) and divide it between five bowls: colour pale pink, dark pink, emerald, ivory and lilac respectively. Prepare a paper piping bag of each colour of icing. Pipe dots of each colour randomly over the space above the powder box. Leave to dry, then pipe some more dots over the top until the space is filled with dots.

29 Use the remaining golden-brown soft-peak icing to pipe lines down the powder box. Leave to dry.

30 Paint the box with a mixture of Antique Gold lustre dust and clear alcohol.

CLUTCH BAG

31 Colour a portion of soft-peak royal icing with a touch of ivory food colour and leave some of the icing white. Add a few drops of pre-boiled, cold water to some of the ivory and white icing to make a run-out consistency (see page 17). Fill four paper piping bags with the different icings.

32 Pipe the outline of the bag, the bow and the quilted detailing with the white soft-peak icing.

33 For the quilted effect, flood alternate squares with the cream run-out icing then leave these to dry. Flood the remaining squares with the same icing and leave to dry completely.

34 Flood inside the outline of the bow with white run-out icing and leave to dry.

35 Make up some icing that is slightly softer than soft-peak (see page 17) and colour it with ivory paste food colour. Prepare a piping bag with the ivory-coloured icing and pipe flowers and swirls over the bow. Pipe a small dot of royal icing at the corner of each quilted square to finish.

HAND MIRROR

36 Colour a portion of soft-peak royal icing with a small touch of black food colour, then add a few drops of pre-boiled, cold water to the grey icing to make a run-out consistency (see page 17).

37 Use the template to pipe the mirror outline with grey icing, then pipe another circle 5mm (¼") outside the first. Pipe a thick U-shape under the outer circle: either pipe two thinner lines and fill them in, or snip off the end of the bag to make a bigger hole. Pipe the outline of the handle and the decorative details.

38 Flood inside the handle and the lines around the mirror with run-out consistency icing. Leave to dry.

39 Add a little water to the soft-peak icing to make it softer, prepare a paper piping bag with the icing and pipe the decorative details over the mirror, using the template as a guide. Leave to dry.

40 Moisten the centre of the mirror with a very small amount of edible glue, then cover it with silver leaf. Paint over the piped details with a mixture of Silver lustre dust and clear alcohol.

SALTED MAPLE BUTTON BISCUITS

INGREDIENTS

30g (1oz) unsalted butter, softened

A pinch of sea salt

20g (¾oz) brown sugar

30g (1oz) maple syrup

15ml (½fl oz) milk

120g (4¼oz) plain flour

EQUIPMENT

Basic equipment (see pages 8–11)

Round cutters: 2.5cm and 4cm
(1" and 1¾")

Small piping nozzle (plain)

MAKES 30 BUTTON BISCUITS

1 Mix the butter, sea salt and brown sugar until well combined. Add the maple syrup and mix.

2 Add the milk and mix again. Fold in the plain flour.

3 Once all the ingredients are combined, wrap the dough in cling film and rest in the fridge for 30 minutes.

4 Roll out the dough to 4mm (³/₁₆") thick using the same method as for the vanilla biscuits on page 14. Chill the sheet of biscuit dough in the fridge for one hour until firm.

5 Remove the dough from the fridge and cut out 30 circles using a 4cm (1¾") round cutter, then emboss a

circle just inside the outer edge with a 2.5cm (1") cutter. Make two or four tiny holes in the centre of each biscuit using a small piping nozzle.

6 Bake the biscuits at 170°C/340°F/gas mark 3½ for 16–20 minutes.

TOP TIP

If you are making these biscuits for favours or as a gift, thread a narrow ribbon through several biscuits and tie in a bow before wrapping in tissue paper or cellophane.

BITTER CHOCOLATE ALMOND COOKIES

INGREDIENTS

55g (2oz) pure cocoa powder
230g (8¼oz) plain flour
230g (8¼oz) unsalted butter, softened
100g (3½oz) icing sugar
70g (2½oz) ground almonds
20ml (¾fl oz) milk

EQUIPMENT

Basic equipment (see pages 8–11)

MAKES APPROXIMATELY 60 MINI COOKIES, 40 MEDIUM-SIZED COOKIES OR 15 HEART-SHAPED COOKIES

1 Preheat the oven to 180°C/350°F/gas mark 4.

2 Sieve the cocoa powder and flour together into a bowl.

3 In another bowl, cream the butter and icing sugar together until pale in colour.

4 Add the dry ingredients little by little to the creamed butter and sugar, then finally add the milk. Combine the ingredients together but be careful not to over-mix them.

5 Once a dough is formed, wrap it in cling film and leave it to rest in the fridge for an hour.

6 Depending on the size and shape of your cookies, baking times will vary from 10–13 minutes. Refer to the projects in this chapter for specific instructions on how to cut, shape and bake the cookie dough.

MONOGRAM SEAL COOKIES

EDIBLES

1 x bitter chocolate almond cookie recipe
(see page 61)
150g (5¼oz) white modelling chocolate (Cocoform)
Confectioners' glaze, IPA (SK)

EQUIPMENT

Basic equipment (see pages 8–11)
Wax seal
Glaze cleaner (SK)

MAKES APPROXIMATELY 60 SMALL MONOGRAM COOKIES

1 Once rested, remove the cookie dough from the fridge. Unwrap it and cut it into four equal portions.

2 Knead the dough slightly until it is soft enough to roll out. Use the palms of your hands to roll out each piece of dough into a long sausage shape. Alternatively, wrap the dough in cling film, twist up the ends, then roll it up and down on the work surface to make a sausage shape.

3 Place the dough on a tray lined with baking paper or cling film and leave it to chill in the fridge for 30 minutes to an hour.

4 Once set, remove the dough from the fridge and use a large, sharp knife to cut the sausages into 1cm (³/₈") thick

pieces. Place the pieces on a tray lined with baking paper, leaving space between each one to allow for spreading. Bake in the oven at 180°C/350°F/gas mark 4 for 10–12 minutes, then leave to cool on a wire rack.

5 Roll some white modelling chocolate into a 1cm (³/₈") diameter ball and flatten the centre of the ball with your finger. Brush the wax seal with confectioners' glaze to sterilize it, then press into the centre of the modelling chocolate. Melt the back of the stamped paste on a warm baking tray then stick it on top of a cookie. Alternatively, you can use a little melted chocolate or some edible glue to attach the seal to the cookies. Once you have finished with the wax seal, remove the confectioners' glaze with some glaze cleaner.

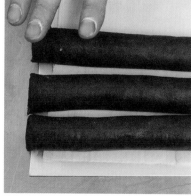
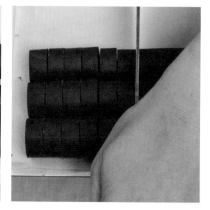

As the chocolate cookie dough is very soft, you can simply roll it into small balls and bake for 10–12 minutes if you are short of time. Sprinkle with icing sugar to serve.

DIAMANT (DIAMOND) COOKIES

EDIBLES

1 x bitter chocolate almond cookie recipe
(see page 61)

50g (1¾oz) granulated or caster sugar

EQUIPMENT

Basic equipment (see pages 8–11)

MAKES APPROXIMATELY 40 SPARKLY COOKIES

1 Once rested, remove the dough from the fridge. Unwrap it and cut it in half, so you have two portions that are approximately 350g (12¼oz) each.

2 Knead the dough slightly until it is soft enough to roll out. Use the palms of your hands to roll out each piece of dough into a long sausage shape. Alternatively, wrap the dough in cling film, twist up the ends and roll it up and down on the work surface to make a sausage shape.

3 Place the dough on a tray lined with baking paper or cling film and leave it to chill in the fridge for 30 minutes to an hour.

4 Sprinkle plenty of granulated sugar or caster sugar on a sheet of baking paper. Remove the dough from the fridge and unwrap it if you have used cling film. Brush both sausages with cooled, boiled water and roll them in the sugar until they are completely covered.

5 Use a sharp knife to cut the sausages into 1cm (³⁄₈") thick cookies. Place the cookies on a tray lined with baking paper, leaving space between each one to allow for spreading.

6 Bake in the oven at 180°C/350°F/gas mark 4 for 10–12 minutes, then leave to cool on a wire rack.

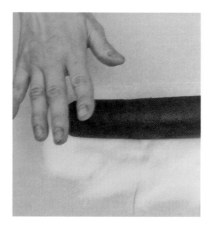

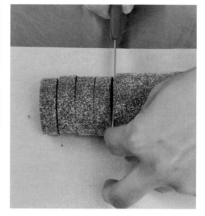

CROSS-STITCH COOKIES

EDIBLES

1 x bitter chocolate almond cookie recipe
(see page 61)

½ x royal icing recipe (see page 16)

Liquid food colour: rose pink

EQUIPMENT

Basic equipment (see pages 8–11)

Heart cookie cutter

Piping nozzles: nos. 1, 2

MAKES APPROXIMATELY 15 HEART-SHAPED COOKIES

1 Roll out the dough to 4mm (³/₁₆") thick using the same method as for the vanilla biscuits on page 14. Chill the sheet of cookie dough in the fridge for one hour until firm.

2 Remove the dough from the fridge and cut out approximately 15 heart shapes with the cutter. If the shapes are firm enough to lift, place them onto a baking tray lined with baking paper. If they are too soft, chill them in the fridge until they firm up.

3 Bake in the oven at 180°C/350°F/gas mark 4 for 10–13 minutes and allow to cool completely on a wire rack before decorating.

4 Make up some royal icing to soft-peak consistency (see page 17) and add a touch of rose pink liquid food colour to make a pale pink shade. Fit a piping bag with a no. 2 nozzle, fill ²/₃ with the icing and pipe a heart outline approximately 1cm (³/₈") in from the edge of the cookie. Pipe another heart shape approximately 1cm (³/₈") inside the first piped heart.

5 Add a little pre-boiled, cold water to the icing to make a run-out consistency (see page 17) and place it in a paper piping bag. Snip the tip off the end of the bag and fill the space between the two heart outlines. Leave to dry.

6 Prepare some more royal icing so it is slightly softer than soft-peak consistency (see page 17). Fit a piping bag with a no. 1 nozzle and fill ⅔ with the softer, white icing. Working inside the heart shape, pipe approximately 25 horizontal lines then leave them to dry for approximately five minutes. Pipe 30 vertical lines over the horizontal lines to create a cross-stitch effect. Leave to dry.

TOP TIP

If you make a mistake when piping the lines, simply remove the icing with a fine paintbrush.

7 For the border, use a no. 1 nozzle and some soft-peak icing to pipe small arches around the outside of the flooded heart shape. Pipe three smaller arches over the top of each larger arch.

8 Add a little water to the softer icing to make it dot consistency (see page 17) then use a no. 1 nozzle to pipe dots around the edge of the pink heart and over each small arch. Fill in some of the squares inside the heart to create a symmetrical cross-stitch design, following the picture as a guide.

You can adapt the method above to create your own variation on the embroidered heart pattern, using the designs shown here for inspiration.

STENCILLED COOKIES

1 For an alternative stencilled design, colour some soft-peak royal icing with your chosen liquid food colours, then pipe the outline of the heart inside each cookie.

2 Use run-out consistency icing in the same colour to flood the heart and leave to dry.

3 Pipe a dot design around the edge of the heart and sprinkle caster sugar over the icing while it's still wet to add sparkle.

4 Place the template of your choice (or make your own from a piece of acetate) onto the iced cookie and spread some soft-peak icing over the stencil with a palette knife. Carefully remove the stencil to reveal your design.

Although the recipes in this chapter vary, if you look closely at the methods you'll see there are only two ways to make a sponge. The easiest way is to use a raising agent such as baking powder, which makes the sponge more stable and is best for rich, flavoured cakes like Victoria sandwiches. The other method is to use whipped egg whites to add volume to the mixture, which means working quickly to keep the air in but gives a lighter end result.

SPONGE
CAKES

VICTORIA SPONGE CAKE

INGREDIENTS

400g (14oz) unsalted butter, softened

400g (14oz) caster sugar

400g (14oz) whole eggs (approx. 8 medium eggs)

400g (14oz) self-raising flour, sieved

EQUIPMENT

Basic equipment (see pages 8–11)

2 x 20.5cm (8") round cake tins

MAKES A 20.5CM (8") ROUND VICTORIA SPONGE

1 Preheat the oven to 180°C/350°F/gas mark 4. Lightly grease the inside of the cake tins with butter, place a circle of greaseproof paper in the base of the tin and line the sides with a strip of paper that is big enough to cover the height and circumference of the tin.

TOP TIP

For best results with this recipe, divide the mixture into two cake tins of the same size: this will reduce the baking time compared to one large cake and you will find that the sponge comes out much lighter. If you do not have two tins the same size, I would recommend that you bake half the mixture at a time.

2 Place the softened butter and caster sugar into an electric mixer with a paddle attachment, then beat on a fast speed until fluffy. Add your choice of flavour at this stage (see the flavour variations opposite).

3 When the mixture becomes light and fluffy, reduce the mixer speed to medium and add the eggs gradually. If the mixture begins to separate, add a spoonful of flour to help the mixture combine.

4 Reduce the mixer speed to low and add the rest of the flour to the bowl, gradually folding it into the mixture.

5 Using a spatula, scrape off the mix from the side and bottom of the bowl, then mix it through again.

6 Divide the mixture evenly between the prepared cake tins (or baking trays) and bake in the preheated oven for 30–40 minutes or until the surface becomes golden brown in colour. When you touch the top of the cake gently it should spring back, or a clean skewer or kitchen knife inserted into the centre should come out clean.

7 Allow the cake to cool in the tin for 10 minutes before taking it out. Leave it on a wire rack until the bottom of the sponge is completely cool.

STORAGE

Wrap the cakes in cling film so they are completely covered. The sponge should last for three to four days at room temperature or for a couple of weeks in the freezer.

FLAVOUR VARIATIONS

VANILLA: add the seeds from one vanilla pod.

ORANGE: add the zest from three oranges.

LEMON: add the zest from four lemons.

CHOCOLATE: replace ¼ of the self-raising flour with an equal amount of cocoa powder and water. For example, for a 400g (14oz) flour recipe, use 300g (10½oz) self-raising flour + 100g (3½oz) cocoa powder and 100ml (3½fl oz) water.

COFFEE: add 75ml (4tbsp) of coffee extract or 50:50 instant coffee dissolved with hot, boiled water. Heat the coffee and water in a microwave for a few seconds to ensure that the coffee granules have completely dissolved.

Multiples of Victoria sponge recipe

Round	10cm (4")	12.5cm (5")	15cm (6")	18cm (7")	20.5cm (8")	23cm (9")	25.5cm (10")	28cm (11")	30.5cm (12")
Square	7.5cm (3")	10cm (4")	12.5cm (5")	15cm (6")	18cm (7")	20.5cm (8")	23cm (9")	25.5cm (10")	28cm (11")
Multiple of recipe	¼	⅓	½	¾	1	1¼	1¾	2¼	2½
Baking time	10+ mins	15+ mins	15+ mins	20+ mins	30+ mins	40+ mins	45+ mins	50+ mins	50+ mins

CUPCAKES

INGREDIENTS

80g (2¾oz) salted butter, softened

200g (7oz) plain flour

250g (8¾oz) caster sugar

1tbsp baking powder

2 large eggs

200ml (7fl oz) whole milk

EQUIPMENT

Basic equipment (see pages 8–11)

12-hole cupcake tin

12 cupcake cases

MAKES 12 MEDIUM-SIZED CUPCAKES

1 Preheat the oven to 180°C/350°F/gas mark 4.

2 Place the butter and all the dry ingredients (including any additional flavourings) in the bowl of a stand mixer, then mix with the paddle attachment at medium speed until it forms a crumble-like texture.

3 Add the eggs and milk to the mixture and mix on a low speed until thoroughly combined. Scrape down the sides of the bowl, turn up the mixer to medium speed and beat until it is smooth and lump-free.

TOP TIP

If preferred you can use self-raising flour instead of plain flour and omit the baking powder.

4 Place the cupcake cases in the wells of the tray and spoon the mixture into each of the cases until they are ⅔ full. Bake in the oven for 15–20 minutes, then turn the tray around and bake for a further five minutes. The cupcakes are baked when they bounce back to the touch or a skewer inserted comes out clean.

5 Leave to cool on a wire rack. Store them in an airtight container and consume within two days.

FLAVOUR VARIATIONS

VANILLA: add the seeds from one-and-a-half vanilla pods.

ORANGE: add the zest from an orange.

LEMON: add the zest from two lemons.

SUGAR SYRUP

INGREDIENTS

500g (1lb 1¾oz) caster sugar
500ml (17fl oz) water

EQUIPMENT

Basic equipment (see pages 8–11)

MAKES 1L (1PT 15FL OZ) SUGAR SYRUP

1 Place the water in a clean saucepan and pour the sugar over it. Bring the syrup to the boil and make sure all the sugar dissolves completely. Clean down the sides of the pan using a clean pastry brush and a little water.

2 Store in an airtight container in the fridge for up to three weeks.

FLAVOUR VARIATIONS

Take the syrup out of the fridge when you need it and add your favourite flavour to complement the cake. The following quantities are for 200ml (7¼fl oz) of sugar syrup.

VANILLA: add the seeds from ½ a vanilla pod.

ORANGE: add the juice from an orange.

LEMON: add the juice from a lemon.

COFFEE: add 10ml (¼fl oz) of instant coffee or coffee liqueur.

CHERRY: add 10ml (¼fl oz) of kirsch (cherry brandy).

BASIC BUTTERCREAM

INGREDIENTS

250g (8¾oz) unsalted butter, softened
250g (8¾oz) icing sugar

MAKES 500G (1LB 1¾OZ) BUTTERCREAM

1 Place the butter and icing sugar in the bowl of an electric mixer and beat with a paddle attachment until soft and fluffy in texture.

2 The buttercream will keep for a couple of days at room temperature, up to two days in the fridge or up to a month in the freezer.

FLAVOUR VARIATIONS

The following flavours can be used for every 500g (1lb 1¾oz) of buttercream filling.

CHOCOLATE: add 250g (8¾oz) of melted chocolate. I recommend using chocolate with over 60% cocoa solids or cocoa mass to get a rich flavour (on all cakes except children's cakes).

ORANGE: add the zest of one to two oranges.

LEMON OR LIME: add the zest of two to three lemons or limes.

VANILLA: add the seeds from ½ a vanilla pod.

COFFEE: add 30ml (2tbsp) of coffee extract.

GREEN TEA: add 30ml (2tbsp) of green tea extract by mixing 10ml (2tsp) of good-quality green tea powder with 20ml (4tsp) of boiled water.

WHIPPED CREAM

For most of the recipes in this book, I use either double cream with 45% milk fat or whipping cream with 35% milk fat. The milk fat content is important for whipped cream, because if it isn't high enough it won't form a fluffy texture.

You can make whipped cream with a hand whisk or in a stand mixer with a whisk attachment. When using a stand mixer, I usually stop whisking the cream just before it forms soft peaks and finish whisking it by hand. Be careful not to over-whisk, otherwise the cream will become grainy as the fat breaks apart from the liquid and starts to turn into butter.

Chantilly cream is whipped cream sweetened with icing sugar. The amount of icing sugar you need should be approximately 10% of the total amount of cream you are using. Add the seeds from a vanilla pod or the zest of some citrus fruit to give the cream extra flavour.

TOP TIP

If the room is very hot, chill the bowl over some ice whilst you are whipping the cream.

ITALIAN MERINGUE BUTTERCREAM

INGREDIENTS

120g (4¼oz) egg white (approx. 4 medium egg whites)

260g (9oz) caster sugar

60ml (2fl oz) water

450g (1lb) unsalted butter, softened

Italian meringue buttercream has a light texture and flavour and can be kept at room temperature for a few hours. As it is very light in colour, it is ideal when you want to create a colourful filling or topping.

MAKES APPROX. 800G (1LB 12OZ) BUTTERCREAM

1 Place the egg whites in the bowl of an electric mixer fitted with a whisk attachment. Whisk the egg whites on a high speed until they start to form soft peaks. Add 20g (¾oz) of caster sugar and continue to mix to create a stiff-peak meringue.

2 Make some sugar syrup with the remaining 240g (8½oz) of caster sugar and the water (see page 75). Heat the syrup to 115–118°C.

3 As soon as the syrup reaches the correct temperature, slowly pour it onto the meringue mixture and mix gently on a low speed. Turn the speed up high and continue to whisk the meringue until it cools down. Place in a container and cover with cling film.

4 Beat the butter in an electric mixer with a paddle attachment, then add the Italian meringue mixture little by little. Mix until the buttercream is smooth in texture.

5 Cover with cling film and store in the fridge for up to two days or freeze for up to two weeks.

TOP TIP

If you don't have a digital thermometer, take a little syrup on a spoon and drop it into some iced water. It is ready to use if you can form the syrup into a soft ball shape with your fingers.

PÂTE À BOMBE BUTTERCREAM

INGREDIENTS

120g (4¼oz) egg yolks (approx. 6–8 medium egg yolks)
190g (6¾oz) caster sugar
70ml (2½fl oz) water
450g (1lb) unsalted butter, softened

MAKES APPROX. 800G (1LB 12OZ) BUTTERCREAM

This buttercream is used in the Gâteau Opéra recipe on page 92 and is light in texture, rich in flavour and is slightly yellowy in colour. It is best to make at least half the recipe as the ingredients may not mix together well in smaller amounts; if you have some leftover, you could use it to fill macaroons or pipe onto cupcakes.

1 Place the egg yolks in the bowl of an electric mixer fitted with a whisk attachment. Whisk the egg yolks on a high speed until they appear light in colour.

2 Make some sugar syrup with the caster sugar and water (see page 75). Heat the syrup to 115–118°C.

3 As soon as the syrup reaches the correct temperature, slowly pour it onto the egg yolks and mix carefully on a low speed. Turn the speed up high and continue to whisk the pâte à bombe mixture until it cools down. Place in a container and cover with cling film.

4 Beat the butter in an electric mixer with the paddle attachment, then add the pâte à bombe little by little. Mix until the buttercream is smooth in texture.

5 Store in the fridge for up to two days.

TOP TIP

If you don't have a digital thermometer, take a little syrup on a spoon and drop it into some iced water. It is ready to use if you can form the syrup into a soft ball shape with your fingers.

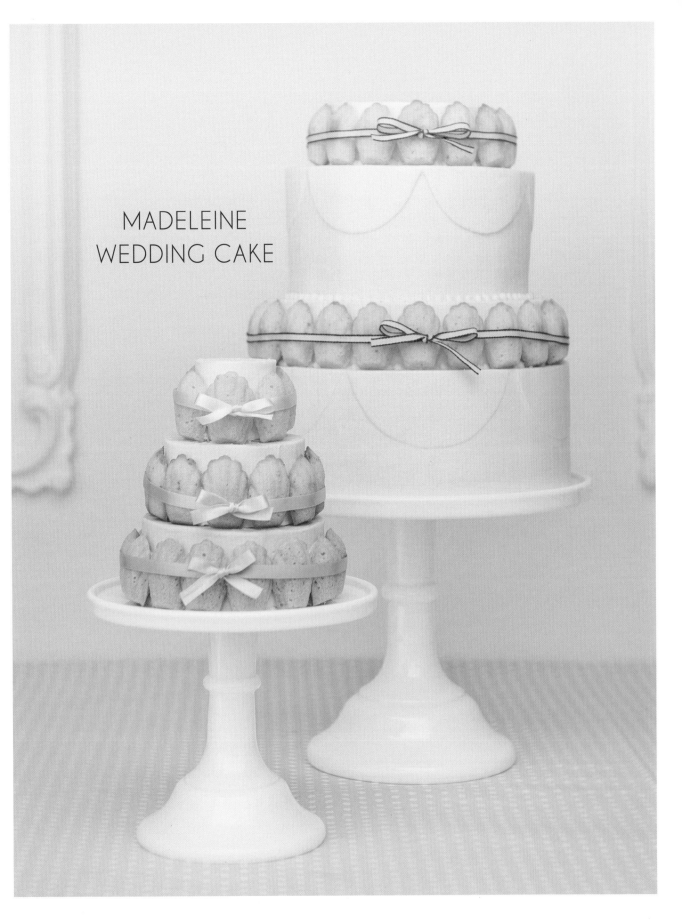

MADELEINE
WEDDING CAKE

MADELEINE WEDDING CAKE

EDIBLES

Cakes

12.5cm (5") round cake, ½ x lemon Victoria sponge recipe baked in one tin (see pages 72–73)

18cm (7") round cake, 1 x lemon Victoria sponge recipe baked in two tins (see pages 72–73)

20.5cm (8") round cake, ½ x lemon Victoria sponge recipe baked in one tin (see pages 72–73)

23cm (9") round cake, 1 x lemon Victoria sponge recipe baked in two tins (see pages 72–73)

150ml (5¼fl oz) lemon-flavoured syrup (see page 75)

1.5kg (3lb 5oz) lemon-flavoured buttercream (see page 75)

250g (8¾oz) lemon curd

Food colour pen: any colour

Madeleines

110g (3¾oz) unsalted butter, plus extra for greasing

100g (3½oz) egg whites (approx. 3 medium egg whites)

100g (3½oz) icing sugar

40g (1½oz) plain flour

40g (1½oz) ground almonds

EQUIPMENT

Basic equipment (see pages 8–11)

Round cake cards: 10cm, 15cm, 18cm and 20.5cm (4", 6", 7" and 8")

Cake leveller (optional)

Large spare cake board

Non-slip mat (optional)

Straight edge

Side scraper

20-hole silicone madeleine mould

Round cutters or cake tins: 7.5cm, 12.5cm and 15cm (3", 5" and 6")

12 cake dowels

Small spirit level (optional)

Cake stand of your choice

Decorative ribbon in a colour of your choice

TOP TIP

Prepare all the sponges the day before, or make sure they have been chilled for a few hours before you need them.

MAKES ONE FOUR-TIER CAKE AND APPROX. 50 SMALL MADELEINES

BASE AND THIRD TIERS

1 Flip the 18cm and 23cm (7" and 9") lemon sponge cakes over and slice the crust off the bottom with a large, serrated knife. Use a cake leveller to cut each 18cm and 23cm (7" and 9") cake into two equal layers, so you have two cakes with four layers of equal thickness.

TOP TIP

If you do not have a cake leveller, measure the height of the cake with a ruler. Make a mark at the halfway point with a knife and use this as a guide to slice it into two equal layers.

2 As the lemon sponges should be pale cream in colour, trim the crusts from around the edge. To do this, place a 20.5cm (8") cake card on one of the 23cm (9") sponge layers then cut around it using a serrated knife. Repeat for the remaining three layers of the 23cm (9") cake. Using a 15cm (6") round cake card, remove the crust from the 18cm (7") third tier cake in the same way.

3 Place a large cake board on top of a turntable, then put a square of greaseproof paper on top of the board. Place the 20.5cm (8") cake card on the greaseproof paper and spread a small amount of buttercream filling over the centre of the card. Position the first layer of the larger base tier centrally on the card.

TOP TIP

The layer of greaseproof paper underneath the cake will make it easier to move the cake once it is iced. If you find that the cake is sliding around on the paper, put a small piece of non-slip mat under the cake card to keep it in place.

4 Brush some lemon-flavoured syrup over the first layer of sponge to keep it moist, then spread a thin layer of lemon buttercream over the top. Place a second layer on sponge on top, brush with syrup and spread a thin layer of lemon curd over the sponge. Place the third layer on top, brush with syrup and spread with buttercream. Position the final layer of sponge on top and brush with syrup.

5 Use a palette knife to spread an even layer of buttercream over the top and sides of the base tier. Pull a straight edge across the top of the cake to level out the icing. Remove any excess from the sides of the cake with a scraper. Leave the cake to chill in the fridge until the buttercream is firm.

6 Remove the cake from the fridge and repeat step 5, spreading even layers of buttercream onto the cake until you have created a smooth covering. Place the cake in the freezer for 10 minutes until the surface has set completely.

7 Measure the height of the cake and cut a strip of greaseproof paper to the same size. Wrap the paper around the cake then cut the strip to approximately 2cm (¾") longer than the circumference to allow for the join. Check that the paper fits around the cake exactly as it will need to be accurate.

8 Fold the paper into six equal sections, leaving 2cm (¾") spare at one end. Use a food colour pen to draw a curve from the corner to the edge of the folded paper then cut along the line neatly with scissors. Open up the scalloped paper with the points facing up and wrap it around the cake so the ends overlap by 2cm (¾"). The paper should stick to the surface as the buttercream will have melted slightly.

9 Spread an even layer of buttercream over the sides of the cake only, then remove any excess with a scraper. Remove any excess from around the top of the cake with a small knife. Leave it to set in the freezer for five minutes. Repeat the process again until the scalloped design is approximately 3–4mm (⅛– ³/₁₆") thick, making sure the surface of the design is smooth. Remove the paper template and leave the cake to set in the fridge.

10 Repeat steps 3–9 for the third tier cake.

TOP AND SECOND TIERS

11 Cut the 12.5cm and 20.5cm (5" and 8") cakes into two layers using a cake leveller or a serrated knife. Trim the crusts from the layers as before using 10cm and 18cm (4" and 7") cake cards. Place the cakes on the corresponding-sized cake cards, then layer and fill with lemon-flavoured buttercream. Repeat steps 5–6 to cover the cakes with buttercream.

MADELEINES

12 Place a pan over a low heat, add the butter and gently swirl the pan as the butter starts to melt. Heat until the butter turns brown: when the butter bubbles at the top, it will start to turn brown on the bottom and is known as *beurre noisette*. Remove from the heat and leave to cool down before use.

13 Whisk the egg whites and the icing sugar together thoroughly but stop just before they start to peak.

14 Mix the flour and ground almonds together and add to the mixture.

15 Add the cooled beurre noisette and mix well.

16 Place the madeleine mix in a clean bowl and cover the surface with cling film. Alternatively, place the mix in a large plastic piping bag. Leave to set in the fridge overnight and use the mix within two to three days.

17 Preheat the oven to 180°C/350°F/ gas mark 4. Grease inside the wells of the madeleine mould with a little softened butter. If you are using a silicone madeleine mould, you do not need to grease the mould.

18 Place the madeleine mix in a large plastic piping bag if you haven't done so already and pipe the mix almost to the top of each well.

19 Bake for five minutes, then turn the tray around and bake for another five minutes. Once baked, the top of the madeleines should spring back to the touch or a skewer inserted

in the centre will come out clean. If necessary, bake for a couple more minutes then remove from the oven and leave to cool on a wire rack.

ASSEMBLY

20 Remove the base tier from the fridge and place a 15cm (6") round cake tin or a greaseproof paper template of the same size on top of the cake. Score around it gently and mark four equally spaced dowel points inside the circle, following the picture opposite as a guide.

21 Insert the first dowel into one of the points and use a food colour pen to make a mark on the dowel just higher than the cake. Remove and cut to size with a serrated knife. Cut three more dowels to exactly the same length, using the first dowel as a guide.

22 Insert the dowels at the marked points on the cake and place a spare cake board on top. Place a small spirit level on top of the board to make sure the dowels are all the same height.

23 Repeat for the second and third tiers, using a cutter or template that is approximately 2.5cm (1") smaller than the cake that will sit on top. You do not need to dowel the top tier.

24 Position the base tier on a cake stand of your choice and check it with a small spirit level if you have one. Stack the cakes on top of one another. If there is space between the tiers, use some leftover buttercream to fill the gaps.

25 Before you attach the madeleines, fill a plastic piping bag with some leftover buttercream and pipe dots around the base of each tier.

26 Starting at the front of the second and top tiers, attach the pre-baked madeleines around the cakes using buttercream. If you find that the madeleines have puffed up too much, trim a little bit off to make them all the same. Tie a ribbon around the madeleines to help them stay in place.

A smaller three-tiered cake with madeleines around each layer would be perfect for a more intimate wedding ceremony or celebration. Add a touch of liquid food colour to the madeleine mix and coordinate the colour of the ribbon to the colour of the sponge.

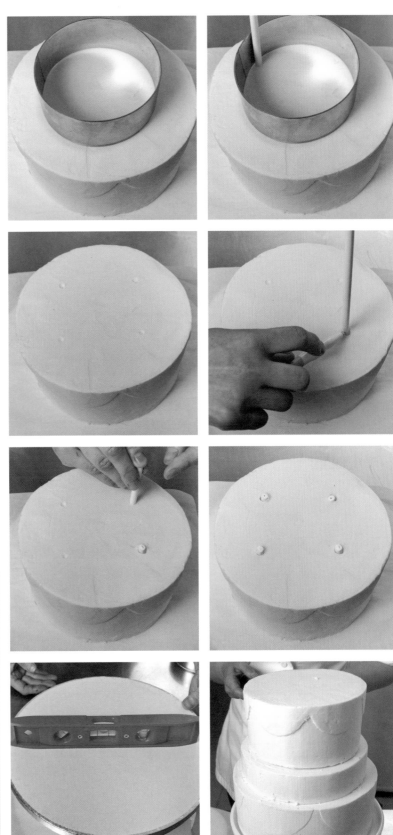

PATTERNED SWISS ROLLS

INGREDIENTS

Sponge

60g (2oz) egg yolks (approx. 3 large egg yolks)

20g (¾oz) caster sugar

30ml (1fl oz) vegetable oil

30ml (1fl oz) water

¼ vanilla pod

75g (2½oz) plain flour

Liquid food colours: green, red

Meringue

3 egg whites

40g (1½oz) caster sugar

Filling

80ml (2¾fl oz) double cream

Cherry/apple patterns:

Sugar syrup, flavoured with kirsch (see page 75)

A selection of fruit cut into strips, e.g. mango, kiwi, banana, strawberries

Coffee extract

Checked pattern:

Sugar syrup, flavoured with coffee liqueur (see page 75)

Walnuts, chopped

Caramel (optional)

EQUIPMENT

Basic equipment (see pages 8–11)

23cm (9") square baking tray

Templates (see pages 198–200)

2 mixing bowls

MAKES A 23CM (9") LONG PATTERNED SWISS ROLL

SPONGE SHEET

1 Preheat the oven to 170°C/340°F/gas mark 3½.

2 Line a baking tray with greaseproof paper, then slide your chosen template underneath.

3 Whisk the egg yolks and caster sugar for the sponge together until thick and pale.

4 Add the oil, water and seeds from ¼ of a vanilla pod to the mixture and continue to whisk.

5 Add 60g (2oz) of flour and continue to mix until the batter is thick.

OPTION A: CHERRY/APPLE PATTERN

6a Take two clean bowls and place a tablespoon of the batter into each one. Add a few drops of the red and green liquid colours into each bowl respectively.

7a Whisk one egg white in a clean mixing bowl with a pinch of caster sugar until light and fluffy.

8a Add 2tbsp of the meringue mixture and ½tbsp of flour to each of the bowls. Fill two paper piping bags with the coloured batter.

9a Following the template, pipe the cherries/apples with the red batter and the leaves with the green batter onto the baking tray.

You can create a variety of different patterns by adapting
this method, but it's always easier when you keep the
design simple. If you're a beginner, the fruity pattern is
a great one to start with then you can move onto the
checked design once you've had a little practice.

10a Place in the oven and bake for 40–50 seconds.

TOP TIP

I recommend that you start preparing the meringue as the piped batter is baking.

OPTION B: CHECKED PATTERN

6b Take two clean bowls and place a tablespoon of the batter into each one. Add a few drops of your chosen colour to each bowl.

7b Whisk one egg white in a mixing bowl with a pinch of caster sugar until light and fluffy.

8b Add 2tbsp of the meringue mixture and ½tbsp of flour or cocoa powder to each of the bowls. Fill two paper piping bags with the coloured batter and snip off the tips of the bags.

9b Pipe the thinner horizontal lines with the darker mixture first. Bake for 30 seconds, then use the same colour batter to pipe the thinner vertical lines intersecting the first using the same colour batter. Bake for another 30 seconds.

10b Pipe over the thicker, horizontal lines in the pattern with the lighter mixture, building up the thicker

sections with several lines of batter. Bake for another 30 seconds, then use the same batter to pipe the thicker, vertical lines intersecting the first. Bake again for 30 seconds.

MERINGUE

11 Add two more egg whites to the remaining uncoloured meringue mixture and whisk until it becomes foamy.

12 Add 40g (1½oz) of caster sugar and continue whisking until stiff peaks form.

13 Take a scoop of the meringue and mix it through the sponge batter with a hand whisk. Add another scoop of meringue and fold it gently into the sponge. Repeat with the remaining meringue. Add 3–4 drops of coffee extract to the batter.

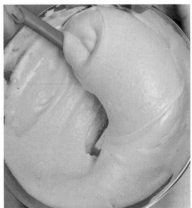

14 Pour the batter into the prepared baking tray over the piped sponge patterns. Spread the mixture evenly and bake in a preheated oven for 13–15 minutes. It is ready when the sponge springs back to the touch or a clean skewer inserted in the centre comes out clean.

15 As soon as the sponge is baked, remove the sponge from the tin and place a clean sheet of baking paper over the top of it. Flip the sponge upside down and peel back the baking paper to check the pattern.

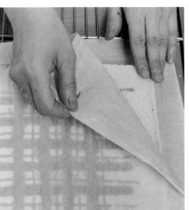

TOP TIP

If you don't want to use the sponge sheet straight away, place a clean piece of baking paper on top of the sponge, wrap it in cling film and freeze for up to a month.

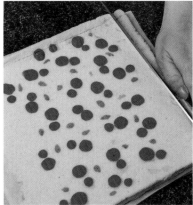

FILLING AND ROLLING

16 Cut the two ends of the sponge sheet at an angle with a large serrated knife, then place the sponge on a lined baking sheet. Brush with flavoured sugar syrup to taste.

17 Whisk the double cream into soft peaks (see page 76) and spread over the sponge sheet, leaving approximately 2cm (¾") uncovered at one end.

18 Arrange the fruit or walnuts in lines horizontally across the sponge sheet, leaving a little space between each line. Pipe lines of caramel across the sponge, if desired.

19 Lift the baking paper at one end and carefully roll up the sponge into a Swiss roll shape. Use a long ruler or straight edge to help you press it into shape. Wrap it up in the remaining baking paper and leave to chill in the fridge for approximately 30 minutes to an hour.

20 For the cherry/apple pattern, paint on the stalks between the fruit and the leaves using a fine paintbrush and some coffee extract to finish.

GÂTEAU OPÉRA

INGREDIENTS

Biscuit Joconde

4 medium eggs

130g (4½oz) icing sugar

30g (1oz) plain flour

130g (4½oz) ground almonds

2–3tsp of coffee granules, diluted in 1tsp of hot, boiled water (optional)

120g (4¼oz) egg white

30g (1oz) caster sugar

30g (1oz) unsalted butter, melted

Ganache for filling

120ml (4¼fl oz) single cream

120g (4¼oz) dark chocolate (53% cocoa solids)

20g (¾oz) glucose syrup

Assembly

120ml (4¼fl oz) coffee-flavoured sugar syrup (see page 75)

¼ x pâte à bombe buttercream recipe (see page 78)

80g (2¾oz) tempered dark chocolate (53% cocoa solids) (see pages 136–137)

150ml (5¼fl oz) Chantilly cream (see page 76)

EQUIPMENT

Basic equipment (see pages 8–11)

2 x 30.5cm (12") square baking tray

8mm (⁵/₁₆") piping nozzle

30.5cm (12") square acetate sheet

MAKES 18 RECTANGULAR GÂTEAUX OPÉRAS

BISCUIT JOCONDE

1 Preheat the oven to 200°C/400°F/gas mark 6.

2 Whisk the four eggs, icing sugar, flour and ground almonds together in a mixer with the whisk attachment until the mixture has a fluffy texture. Add the coffee to the mixture and stir through well.

3 Place the egg whites in a clean bowl and whisk at high speed until they form soft peaks. Add ⅓ of the caster sugar and continue to whisk at high speed until stiff peaks form. Add the rest of the caster sugar little by little.

4 Add ⅓ of the meringue mixture into the cake batter and carefully mix it through using a hand whisk, taking care not to destroy the meringue. Add the melted butter and mix.

5 Add half of the leftover meringue into the mixture and fold it through using a spatula. Add the rest and fold it through.

6 Spread the Joconde mix evenly over two lined baking trays with a large, cranked palette knife. Bake for 10–12 minutes.

7 As soon as the sponge is baked, remove it from the oven and place a clean sheet of baking paper on top of each one. Turn the tray upside down and carefully peel the paper lining off the sponge. Allow to cool on a wire rack.

GANACHE

8 Use the ingredients listed to make a ganache, following steps 3–5 for Earl Grey Tea 'Nama Choco' Ganache (see page 138). As this is a plain ganache, you don't need to infuse the cream.

ASSEMBLY

9 Cut each Joconde sponge sheet lengthways into two equal strips. Place one of the strips on a piece of greaseproof paper and brush ¼ of the sugar syrup over the surface of the sponge. Spread half of the buttercream evenly over the top.

10 Place a second strip of sponge on top and brush with syrup. For best results, leave the gâteau to firm in the freezer for a few minutes.

11 Spread 200g (7oz) of ganache evenly over the top of the second layer and place a third strip of sponge on top. Brush with more sugar syrup and leave it to firm in the freezer for a few minutes.

12 Spread another 80g (2¾oz) of buttercream evenly over the third layer, place the last strip of sponge on top and brush with the remaining syrup. Rest the gâteau in the freezer for a few minutes and spread the remaining chocolate ganache evenly over the top. Allow it to set in the fridge.

13 Trim one end with a large, hot knife to neaten it, then cut the gâteau in half lengthways to make two sections that are approximately 7cm (2¾") wide. Starting from the trimmed end, cut each half of the gâteau into 3cm (1⅛") wide rectangles, so that you get 18 good-sized pieces.

DECORATION

14 Temper the chocolate (see pages 136–137) and spread it thinly over a large sheet of acetate. Leave it to set for a few seconds, then cut it into 7cm x 3cm (2¾" x

1⅛") rectangles with a sharp knife. As soon as you have finished, place the chocolate-coated sheet under a heavy baking tray to keep it flat.

15 Whip some Chantilly cream to form soft peaks for piping. Fit a large plastic piping bag with an 8mm (5/16") round piping nozzle and fill with the whipped cream. Pipe several dots of cream over the top layer of the gâteau, then peel a chocolate rectangle off the acetate and rest it on top of the cream.

TOP TIPS

Although you may only need 80g (2¾oz), it is a good idea to temper nearer 500g (1lb 1¾oz) of chocolate so that the chocolate retains its heat and stays melted as you work.

Pipe the Chantilly cream at the very last minute to keep it fresh; the buttercream and ganache should be served at room temperature for a better taste.

PATTERNED OPÉRA CAKES

INGREDIENTS

Pâte décor

10g (¼oz) unsalted butter, softened

10g (¼oz) icing sugar

7g (¼oz) egg whites (approx. ¼ of an egg white), at room temperature

5g (just under ¼oz) plain, soft flour

10g (¼oz) pure cocoa powder

Sponge

1 x biscuit Joconde recipe (see page 92)

Assembly

60ml (2fl oz) coffee-flavoured sugar syrup (see page 75)

160g (5½oz) pâte à bombe buttercream (see page 78)

250g (8¾oz) dark chocolate ganache for filling (see page 93)

Decoration

200g (7oz) tempered dark chocolate (see pages 136–137)

50g (1¾oz) white Cocoform modelling chocolate

Paste food colours: brown, yellow

Metallic lustre dust food colour: gold

Clear alcohol, e.g. vodka or gin

White vegetable fat

EQUIPMENT

Basic equipment (see pages 8–11)

Pâte décor

2 x 30.5cm (12") square baking trays

Piping nozzle: no. 1.5

Lace pattern template (see page 201)

Assembly

Round cutters: 3cm and 4cm (1⅛" and 1½")

10 x 5.5cm x 3.5cm (2¼" x 1⅜") dessert rings

Decoration

Acetate sheets: 4cm x 15cm (1½" x 6"), 30.5cm (12") square

Long cardboard tube (e.g. from a roll of kitchen paper), cut in half lengthways and wrapped in tin foil

SK Great Impressions Jewel Mould

Textured scraper

SK Great Impressions 7cm (2¾") Feather Mould

MAKES 10 ROUND OPÉRA CAKES

PÂTE DÉCOR

1 Preheat the oven to 200°C/400°F/gas mark 6.

2 Line two 30.5cm (12") square baking trays with baking paper. Copy the lace pattern template onto a piece of

paper, then slide the template underneath the paper lining and position it in the corner of the tray.

3 Cream the softened butter and icing sugar together. Add the egg white gradually and finally fold in the flour and cocoa powder.

4 Fit a paper piping bag with a no. 1.5 nozzle and fill with the pâte décor. Pipe five lace patterns across the width of the tray, following the template. Repeat on the second tray. Place the trays in the freezer to set for half an hour.

5 Spread 1/3 of the biscuit Joconde mixture over the piped patterns. As the lace pattern is very detailed, make sure that the sponge mix fills all the holes in the design. Pour the rest of the Joconde mix over the trays and spread it out evenly with a spatula. Bake the sponges for 10–12 minutes.

ASSEMBLY

6 Cut the sponge sheets into 10 x 3.5cm x 16.5cm (1³/₈" x 6½") strips with a sharp knife, so there is one lace pattern per strip. Cut out 20 circles from each of the leftover sponges using a 3cm (1½") round cutter so you have 40 discs in total.

7 Cut 10 x 3.5cm x 17cm (1³/₈" x 6¾") strips of greaseproof paper and use them to line each dessert ring. Insert the patterned sponge strips into the rings, overlap the join then cut through this with a knife. Remove the ends. Place a sponge disc into the bottom of each ring, then brush the sponge with coffee-flavoured sugar syrup.

8 Place some pâte à bombe buttercream into a piping bag, snip off the tip and pipe approximately 10g (¼oz) into each ring. Place another sponge disc on top and brush with more coffee-flavoured sugar syrup.

9 Place some ganache into a piping bag, snip off the tip and pipe approximately 10g (¼oz) into each ring. Place a third sponge disc on top and brush with some more syrup. Pipe another layer of buttercream on top and finish with another sponge disc. Leave to set in the fridge for 30 minutes then remove from the dessert ring.

DECORATION

10 Temper the dark chocolate (see pages 136–137) and spread some of it thinly over a large sheet of acetate. Leave it to set for a few seconds, then cut out 10 x 4cm (1½") circles using the round cutter. As soon as you have finished, place the chocolate-coated sheet under a heavy baking tray to keep it flat.

11 For the chocolate jewels, pour some more tempered chocolate into the wells of a jewel mould. Leave the chocolate to set in the fridge for approximately 30 minutes. Once set, remove the jewels from the mould and paint with a mixture of clear alcohol and gold lustre dust food colour.

12 For the chocolate curls, spread a small amount of tempered chocolate very thinly over a 4cm x 15cm (1½" x 6") sheet of acetate, then pull a textured scraper down the chocolate to make it stripy. Leave the surface to set slightly, then carefully twist the acetate sheet into a curl. Place it in the centre of half a cardboard tube to help keep its shape, then leave it to set completely. Once set, peel off the acetate sheet and allow the chocolate to curl up.

13 Add a touch of brown and yellow paste food colours to some modelling chocolate (Cocoform). Grease a feather mould with a little white vegetable fat, then fill the mould with approximately 5g (just under ¼oz) of modelling chocolate. Remove the feather from the mould and leave to firm on a piece of kitchen paper. Paint the feather with the gold lustre dust and clear alcohol mixture.

14 Spread a small amount of ganache over the top of each cake and place a chocolate disc on top of each one. Arrange some chocolate curls and a feather decoration on top and secure with a little chocolate ganache. Attach a gold jewel to the front of each cake with a tiny amount of ganache.

TIERED CHARLOTTE CHEESECAKE

EDIBLES

Sponge fingers

2 large eggs, separated

50g (1¾oz) caster sugar

¼ vanilla pod

50g (1¾oz) plain flour, sieved

Icing sugar for dusting

Baked cheesecake

Base

100g (3½oz) digestive biscuits

50g (1¾oz) unsalted butter, melted

Filling

440g (15½oz) soft cream cheese

145g (5oz) caster sugar

45g (1½oz) unsalted butter, softened

¼ vanilla pod

190g (6¾oz) sour cream

120g (4¼oz) eggs (approx. 2 large eggs)

40g (1½oz) egg yolks (approx. 2 large egg yolks)

15g (½oz) cornflour

Assembly

200ml (7fl oz) whipped cream (see page 76)

20g (¾oz) icing sugar

EQUIPMENT

Basic equipment (see pages 8–11)

2–3 large baking trays

1cm (³/₈") round piping nozzle

Round cake tins: 7.5cm, 10cm and 12.5cm (3", 4" and 5")

7.5cm (3") cake card

10cm and 12.5cm (4" and 5") round cake drums

4 plastic dowels

Decorative ribbon in colours of your choice

MAKES 80-90 SPONGE FINGERS AND 7.5CM, 10CM AND 12.5CM (3", 4" AND 5") ROUND CHEESECAKES

This three-tier dessert is a cross between a traditional charlotte russe and a baked cheesecake, making it a delicious, contemporary addition to any sweet table.

SPONGE FINGERS

1 Preheat the oven to 170°C/350°F/gas mark 3½.

2 Line two to three large baking trays with greaseproof paper and fit a large plastic piping bag with a 1cm (³/₈") round nozzle. If you're a beginner, draw two pairs of lines

that are each approximately 8–9cm (3¹/₈–3½") apart across the reverse of the baking paper before lining the trays. You can use them as guidelines when piping to make the fingers a uniform length.

3 Whisk the egg whites in a clean, grease-free electric mixer fitted with a whisk attachment until they form soft peaks. Add a third of the caster sugar and continue to whisk at a high speed until the mixture forms stiff peaks.

4 Add the rest of the sugar and the seeds from ¼ of a vanilla pod and continue to whisk. Add the egg yolks and mix in well.

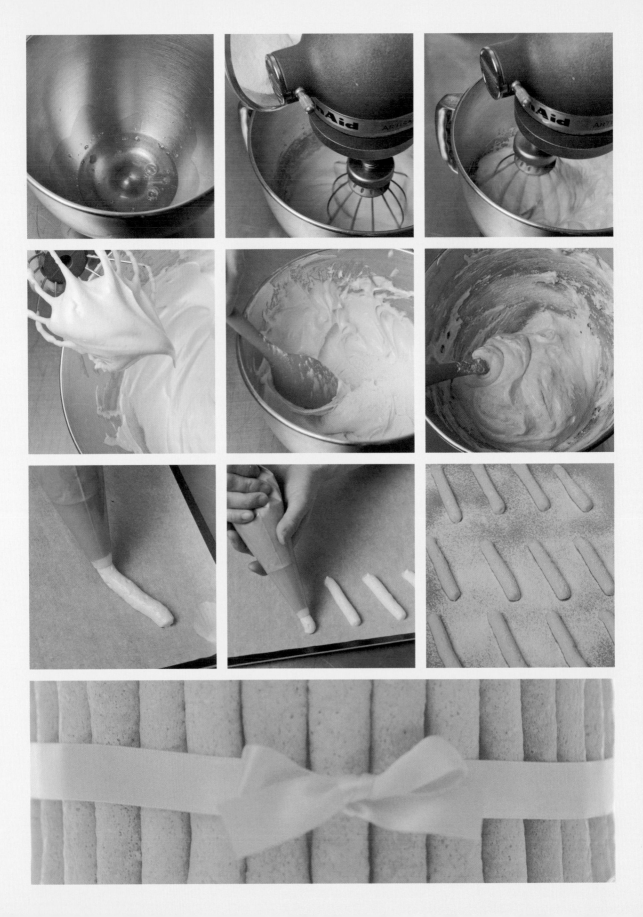

5 Gently fold ⅓ of the sieved flour into the meringue with a large metal serving spoon or balloon whisk. Once it has all combined, add the rest of the flour a little at a time.

6 Transfer all the mixture into the prepared piping bag. Hold the bag at 45° to the lined tray and pipe finger shapes that are 8–9cm (3⅛–3½") long and as wide as the piping nozzle. Leave a 2cm (¾") gap between each biscuit.

7 Once all the fingers are piped, lightly sift icing sugar over the top of them.

8 Bake for nine to 10 minutes until they start to colour. Remove from the oven and leave to cool on a wire rack.

BAKED VANILLA CHEESECAKE

TOP TIP

Instead of using a 7.5cm (3") round cake tin, you could always use a baking cup or a cardboard ice cream tub of the same size.

9 Line the cake tins with baking paper.

10 Place the digestive biscuits in a strong plastic bag and crush them with a rolling pin.

11 Melt the butter in a small pan or microwave. Add the crushed biscuits to the butter and mix through.

12 Transfer some of the mixture into each tin. Press and flatten the biscuit mix into the base of each tin using a flat surface, such as the bottom of a clean drinking glass.

13 Preheat the oven to 180°C/350°F/gas mark 4. Prepare a bain-marie (baking dish or tin filled with water) so that the hot water is approximately 3cm (1⅛") deep.

14 Fit an electric mixer with the paddle attachment and place the soft cheese, butter, seeds from ¼ of a vanilla pod and caster sugar in the bowl. Beat together on a medium speed until creamy in texture. Scrape down the sides of the bowl and the paddle attachment to make sure there are no lumps at this stage.

15 Put the mixer on a low speed and gradually add the sour cream. Mix in at a medium speed.

16 Add the eggs and egg yolks to the mixture a little at a time.

17 Add the cornflour and gently mix it through with a hand whisk. Try not to add too much air to the mixture at this stage.

18 Pour the mix into the prepared cake tins and bake the cheesecakes in a bain-marie as follows:

7.5cm (3") for 40 minutes;

10cm (4") for 50 minutes;

12.5cm (5") for 60 minutes.

Stagger the baking times so that all the cheesecakes will be ready at the same time. Gently shake the tin: the cheesecake is ready if it has a slight wobble and the surface is slightly golden.

19 Once baked, turn off the oven and let the cheesecakes cool down gradually in the oven to prevent the surface from cracking. Once cool, remove from the oven and leave overnight.

TOP TIP

To make a lemon cheesecake, add the finely grated zest of one lemon to the mixture in step 14 and omit the vanilla seeds.

ASSEMBLY

20 Place the cheesecakes on the corresponding-sized cake card or drum. If necessary, trim the smallest cheesecake to size using the 7.5cm (3") cake card as a guide.

21 Whip up the cream to soft-peak consistency and add the icing sugar to taste. Use a cranked palette knife to spread the whipped cream over the top and sides of each cheesecake.

22 Dowel the 12.5cm (5") round cheesecake (see page 84), then stack the cheesecakes on top of one another.

23 Hold one of the sponge fingers against the side of a cheesecake and make a mark on the biscuit 5mm (¼") above the height of the cake. Trim to size, then use this as a guide to cut the remaining sponge fingers to size. If the cheesecakes are uneven depths, cut the fingers to the appropriate size for each tier.

24 Starting at the front, stick the sponge fingers closely together around each cheesecake. Tie a length of ribbon around the sponge biscuits on each tier to help secure them in place.

KARDINALSCHNITTE WREATH

INGREDIENTS

Meringue

50g (1¾oz) egg whites

50g (1¾oz) caster sugar

Sponge

25g (just over ¾oz) whole eggs (approx. ½ medium egg)

15g (½oz) egg yolks (approx. 1 medium egg)

20g (¾oz) caster sugar

20g (¾oz) plain flour, sieved

Icing sugar for dusting

Filling

½ x crème pâtissière recipe (see page 112)

190g (6¾oz) whipping cream (see page 76)

Sliced fresh fruit of your choice (optional)

Decoration

12–15 meringue flowers (see pages 174–177)

EQUIPMENT

Basic equipment (see pages 8–11)

10cm and 18cm (4" and 7") round baking tins, cake cards or drums (to use as templates)

Large baking tray

Savoy piping nozzle: star

This recipe is my take on the traditional Kardinalschnitte (or Cardinal Slice), which is one of my favourite Viennese pastries. It is usually a long, rectangular sponge sandwich with an ice cream filling, but I think the flavour and texture of the sponge also works well with meringue and whipped cream. The wreath shape and meringue flowers prettify this classic dessert.

MAKES A 20.5CM (8") ROUND SPONGE WREATH

MERINGUE

1 Preheat the oven to 200°C/400°F/gas mark 6.

2 Draw around an 18cm (7") round baking tin or cake card on a piece of baking paper, then draw a 10cm (4") circle inside the larger ring. Repeat to make a second template in the same way, then turn the baking paper upside down and place each template on a baking tray.

3 Whisk the egg whites until they form soft peaks. Add ⅓ of the caster sugar for the meringue, whisking continuously. Add the rest of the sugar a little at a time and continue to whisk until it forms a stiff, glossy meringue.

4 Fit a large plastic piping bag with a star nozzle and fill with the meringue mixture. Pipe around the outline of the templates to create two rings.

SPONGE

5 Put the whole eggs, egg yolks and caster sugar in a separate bowl and whisk until the mixture reaches 'ribbon'

stage: when you lift the mixture with a whisk, it should leave a ribbon-like trail for a few seconds before settling back into the mixture.

6 Gently fold through the sieved flour with a spatula.

7 Place the mixture into a piping bag and fill in the space between the inner and outer meringues. Sprinkle icing sugar over the surface of the sponge.

8 Bake for two to three minutes until the surface is slightly coloured, then turn the temperature down to 170°C/350°F/gas mark 3½ and continue to bake for another 20 minutes. Leave to cool on a wire rack.

FILLING

9 Make the crème pâtissière following the recipe on page 112 and leave to cool down completely.

10 Whisk the whipping cream until it forms soft peaks. Add some of the whipped cream to the cold crème pâtissière and whisk until smooth. Add some more whipped cream and check the consistency: if it is too soft, whip up the remaining cream even more and mix in.

11 Fit a large plastic piping bag with a star nozzle and fill with the crème pâtissière mixture. Pipe it around one of the sponge rings, then place some fruit slices on top, if desired. Place the other sponge ring on top.

12 Spread the leftover cream over the surface of the sponge lid and attach the baked meringue flowers.

TOP TIP

You can also pipe the flowers directly onto the wreath with whipped cream (see page 76) instead of meringue, following the instructions for piping buttercream flowers on pages 179–185.

People often think that choux pastry is challenging to make, but when you understand the process it is really quite easy! Once you get the hang of it, you can make a whole range of pretty pastries that are sure to impress at dinner parties and special occasions. It's also quite handy because you can freeze the choux pastry mixture, allowing you to prepare it well in advance.

CHOUX
PASTRY

BASIC CHOUX PASTRY

INGREDIENTS

300ml (10½fl oz) water

120g (4¼oz) butter, cubed
(at room temperature)

A pinch of salt

A pinch of sugar

180g (6¼oz) strong white flour, sieved

5–6 medium eggs

EQUIPMENT

Basic equipment (see pages 8–11)

Plastic piping bag

Piping nozzle of required shape

MAKES 20 CHOUX RINGS, 120-130 SMALL BUNS, 50-60 ÉCLAIRS, 30 SWANS OR 20 SNAKES

1 Place the water, butter and pinch of salt and sugar in a medium-sized saucepan and bring to the boil. Make sure the butter has melted completely.

TOP TIP

It is important that the butter is at room temperature, otherwise the water may evaporate before the butter has a chance to melt completely.

2 Remove the pan from the heat, add the flour and stir in well with a spatula. If you are making more than one quantity of this recipe, you will find it is easier to use a wooden spatula to stir the mixture.

3 Return the pan to the stove on a gentle heat and beat for approximately one minute, until the mixture is formed. (This will take longer if you are making more than one quantity).

4 Put the mixture into a bowl. If you are using an electric mixer, beat slowly with a paddle attachment. Crack four eggs into a small bowl and add them to the mixture slowly, beating continuously. If you are mixing by hand, add the eggs one at a time.

5 Crack the last egg into a small bowl and whisk it roughly. Add half the egg to the mixture and beat it in slowly. Lift some of the mixture with a spatula and tilt it so it drops back into the rest of the mixture. It is ready if it has a smooth, glossy texture which settles back into the mixture slowly (approximately 10 seconds). If it drops off the spatula too quickly it is still too firm: add the rest of the egg little by little and test again until you achieve the right consistency. If it is still too firm, the temperature of the mix may be affecting the consistency so you may need to add another egg.

6 Refer to the projects in this chapter for specific instructions on how to pipe, bake and fill choux pastry.

STORAGE

Choux pastry tastes better fresh but you can freeze the uncooked, piped mixture for up to a month if required: when you are ready to cook the pastry, space the shapes out evenly on a baking tray and leave to defrost completely before baking. You can freeze the unfilled, cooked pastry for up to a week.

CRÈME PÂTISSIÈRE (PASTRY CREAM)

INGREDIENTS

500ml (17½fl oz) milk

80g (2¾oz) egg yolks

125g (4½oz) caster sugar

20g (¾oz) plain flour

20g (¾oz) cornflour

30g (1oz) butter

The basic pastry cream recipe can be adapted easily to make different flavours. Simply add your favourite liqueur or fruit purée, or follow one of the variations given below.

MAKES ENOUGH TO FILL 30 MINI CHOUX BUNS

1 Pour the milk into a large saucepan, bring to the boil gently then remove the pan from the heat.

2 Meanwhile, whisk the egg yolks and caster sugar together in a large mixing bowl until they turn pale in colour. Whisk in the plain flour and cornflour and set aside.

3 Slowly pour ⅓ of the hot milk onto the egg and sugar mixture, whisking constantly, then add the remaining milk and return the mixture to the pan. It is important to whisk the mixture as soon as you pour the milk in to prevent the eggs from scrambling.

4 Bring the mixture back to the boil, whisking continuously. It will start thickening but keep whisking until it reaches a smooth, rich texture.

5 Remove the pan from the heat then add the butter and whisk it into the mixture.

6 Pour the cream into a clean, shallow container and place a piece of cling film over the top to prevent a skin forming. When cool, refrigerate until needed. Use it within two days.

FLAVOUR VARIATIONS

VANILLA: add the seeds from one vanilla pod to the milk in step 1.

CHOCOLATE: melt 200g (7oz) of dark chocolate (50–60% cocoa solids) and add it to the pastry cream at the end. If the mixture is too firm to pipe, soften it by adding some single cream.

CARAMEL: make a caramel by boiling 180g (6¼oz) of caster sugar in a pan. Pour 160ml (5½fl oz) of boiled single cream into the pan, mix then allow to cool. Chill in the fridge then mix the caramel into the basic pastry cream.

COFFEE: add 30ml (2tbsp) of coffee extract to the finished basic pastry cream.

CRÈME DIPLOMAT

For a lighter pastry cream, gradually mix in 380g (13½oz) of whipped cream to the cold crème pâtissière. As a guide for other quantities of crème diplomat, I usually use one part whipped cream to two parts cold pastry cream.

CHOUX RINGS

EDIBLES

1 x choux pastry recipe (see page 110)

2 x crème pâtissière recipe (or 1½ x crème diplomat recipe) (see page 112)

200g (7oz) buttercream (see page 76)

400g (14oz) white modelling chocolate (Cocoform): 300g (10½oz) coloured with violet paste food colour, 100g (3½oz) white

Liquid food colour: mint green

Paste food colour: violet

EQUIPMENT

Basic equipment (see pages 8–11)

Savoy piping nozzle: 1.5cm (⅝") star

Metal skewer

Cake smoother (optional)

MAKES 20 CHOUX RINGS

CHOUX RINGS

1 Draw a series of 8cm (3⅛") diameter circles on several pieces of paper to use as templates, making sure to leave approximately 3–4cm (1½") between each circle. Place each piece of paper onto a baking tray and secure a sheet of baking paper over the top using dots of the mixture in the corners.

2 Fit a plastic piping bag with a star piping nozzle and fill with the choux pastry mixture. Pipe around the outline of each of the circles following the template. Once you have piped over the circles, slide the template along so you can pipe more rings. Remove the template before baking.

3 Bake the choux rings at 220°C/425°F/gas mark 7 for 15 minutes then, once the pastry has puffed up, turn the

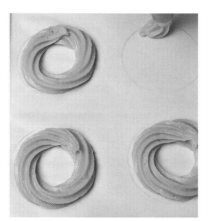

temperature down to 180°C/350°F/gas mark 4. Continue baking for another five to 10 minutes. Do not open the oven door while the pastry is baking.

4 Once the choux rings are golden brown, turn the oven down to 150°C/300°F/gas mark 2 and continue baking for another five to 10 minutes to dry the pastry out.

5 Take one choux ring out of the oven to test it: it is ready if it feels hard to the touch. If the pastry is still soft, leave the rings in the oven for another three to five minutes. Once baked, remove all the rings from the oven and leave to cool on a wire rack.

6 Make three to four evenly spaced holes in the back of each pastry ring with a skewer. Place the crème pâtissière in a plastic piping bag, then cut off the tip with a pair of scissors to make a tiny hole. Pipe cream into the holes in the pastry to fill the ring. Place each choux ring face-up on a tray.

DECORATION

7 Add some mint green liquid food colour to the buttercream and stir it through to get an even colour. Split the buttercream between two paper piping bags.

8 Cut the very tip off one of the bags and pipe a thin, green line back and forth over a ring. Cut the end of the other piping bag into a V-shape then pipe some small leaf shapes randomly over the ring (see page 192).

leave space in between each one. Gently push down on each piece with your hand or a cake smoother to flatten it.

10 Flatten one long side of each sausage of paste, then roll it up from one end to make the centre of the rose. Use your finger to flatten down the top ²/₃ of each small piece to make a petal, leaving the bottom edge of the petal slightly thicker. Wrap three petals around the rose centre with the thicker part of the petal at the base of the rose bud. Cut away any excess paste from the bottom of the flower. Make another two roses in the same way.

11 Knead a small amount of white chocolate modelling paste into the trimmings of purple paste to make it a lighter colour. Roll the lighter paste into a sausage, cut it into thirds and make three slightly larger petals in the same way as before. Wrap the petals around the outside of one of the rose buds to make a larger rose.

12 Repeat steps 9–11 to make two rose buds and one rose for each choux ring. Attach the roses randomly over the top of the choux ring with dots of the green buttercream to finish. Refrigerate before serving.

9 Roll 15g (½oz) of the violet-coloured modelling chocolate into a sausage that is approximately 12cm (4¾") long, then cut it into 12 sections. Roll three pieces into long sausages and place the remaining nine pieces between two sheets of cling film, making sure that you

Choux rings decorated with
royal iced leaves and edible
metallic dragées.

CHOUX SNAKES

EDIBLES

1 x choux pastry recipe (see page 110)

1½ x crème pâtissière recipe (or 1 x crème diplomat recipe) (see page 112)

150g (5¼oz) royal icing (see page 16)

Liquid food colours: dark brown, mint green, orange, pale blue, rose pink, violet, yellow

EQUIPMENT

Basic equipment (see pages 8–11)

Savoy piping nozzle: 1.5cm (⁵⁄₈") round

8 plastic bowls

MAKES 20 CHOUX SNAKES

1 Fit a large plastic piping bag with a 1.5cm (⁵⁄₈") round piping nozzle and fill with the choux pastry mixture. Secure a sheet of baking paper onto a baking tray using dots of mixture in the corners. Pipe the snakes onto the tray: squeeze the bag for one second to make a circle for the head then pipe two or three wavy, 15–18cm (6–7") long lines next to each other to create the snake's body.

TOP TIP

If you are using a silicone-coated baking tray, there is no need to line it with paper before you pipe onto it.

2 Bake them at 220°C/425°F/gas mark 7 for 10–15 minutes. Once the pastry is puffed up, turn down the oven to 180°C/350°F/gas mark 4 and continue to bake for another 10 minutes. Do not open the door whilst the pastry is baking.

3 Once the snakes are golden brown, turn the oven down to 150°C/300°F/gas mark 2 and bake for another five to 10 minutes to dry the pastry out.

4 Take one choux snake out of the oven at this stage and gently press it. If it is hard, take all of the snakes out of the oven and allow to cool on a wire rack. If the pastry is still soft, leave them in the oven at a lower temperature to dry out for another five minutes before checking again.

5 Once cool, make two to three holes in the bottom of each snake in preparation for the filling.

6 Place the crème pâtissière in a plastic piping bag, then cut off the tip with a pair of scissors to make a tiny hole. Fill each of the choux snakes with a small amount of crème pâtissière from the pre-made holes. To keep the filling fresh, make sure you place the snakes in the fridge until you are ready to move onto the next step.

7 Make the royal icing to run-out consistency (see page 17). Place a dessertspoon of royal icing in two bowls, leave one white and colour the other with dark brown liquid food colour. Place tablespoons of royal icing in each of the remaining bowls and colour with pale blue, pink, yellow, green, orange and violet liquid food colours respectively.

8 Place each of the colours into a paper piping bag and snip off the very tips of the bags. Use the white icing to pipe two tiny dots for the eyes then leave to dry slightly. Use the different colours of icing to pipe dots randomly along each snake. Pipe either blue or brown dots on top of the eyes to make the pupils, then pipe a forked tongue with pink icing.

CHOUX SWANS

EDIBLES

½ x choux pastry recipe (see page 110)

½ x crème pâtissière recipe (see page 112)

300g (10½oz) fresh double cream

30g (1oz) icing sugar

EQUIPMENT

Basic equipment (see pages 8–11)

Sheet of paper

Savoy piping nozzle: 1.5cm ($^5/_8$") star

Template (see page 202)

Piping nozzle: no. 3 (optional)

Cocktail stick

MAKES 15 CHOUX SWANS

1 Use the template to draw approximately 20 swan necks onto a sheet of paper, positioning them a few centimetres apart. It is a good idea to make more neck shapes than needed in case of breakages.

2 For the swan bodies, fit a large plastic piping bag with a large star nozzle and fill with the choux pastry mixture. Secure a sheet of baking paper onto a baking tray using dots of mixture in the corners. Pipe 15 teardrop shapes onto the baking sheet, spacing them a few centimetres apart.

3 Bake the swan bodies at 200°C/400°F/gas mark 6 for approximately 10–15 minutes. Once the choux pastry has puffed up, turn down the oven to 180°C/350°F/gas mark 6 and continue baking for five to 10 minutes. Do not open the oven door whilst the pastry is baking.

4 Once the choux buns are golden brown, turn down the oven to 150°C/300°F/gas mark 2 and bake for another five to 10 minutes to dry the pastry out.

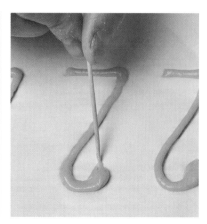

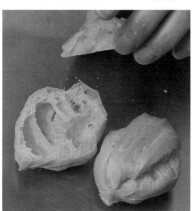

5 Take one swan body out of the oven at this stage and gently press it. If it is hard, take all of the swans out of the oven and allow to cool on a wire rack. If the pastry is still soft, leave them in the oven at a lower temperature to dry out for another five minutes before checking again.

6 Place 2tbsp of the pastry mixture into a small paper piping bag and snip off the tip to make a 5mm (¼") hole (or you could use a no. 3 piping nozzle if you have one). Place the swan neck template on a baking tray, secure a piece of baking paper over the top and pipe over the template. Use a cocktail stick to make a small beak shape at the top of each neck.

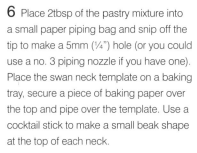

7 Bake the necks at 170°C/340°F/ gas mark 3½ for five minutes, then turn the oven down and continue to bake at 150°C/300°F/gas mark 2 for another five to 10 minutes until the swan necks are hard.

8 Once the bodies have cooled, cut a ⅓ from the top of each one then cut it in half to make two wings. Fill the swan bodies with crème pâtissière until level with the top of the pastry. To keep the filling fresh, make sure you place the swans in the fridge until you are ready to move onto the next step.

9 Whip the double cream and icing sugar together to just before soft-peak stage: softer cream is less likely to split when you pipe it. Fit a large plastic piping bag with a large star nozzle and fill with the whipped cream. Pipe a shell shape along the top of the crème pâtissière filling.

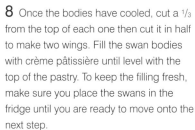

10 Stick the wings either side of the whipped cream and insert a pastry neck at the front so it stands up. Repeat for the remaining choux swans. Dust with some icing sugar for a delicate finish.

COFFEE ÉCLAIRS

EDIBLES

½ x choux pastry recipe (see page 110)

1 x coffee-flavoured crème pâtissière recipe
(see page 112)

Egg wash (one egg yolk + pinch of salt and sugar)

500g (1lb 1¾oz) pack of fondant icing mix (made
up according to the packet instructions)

Coffee extract, to taste

Sugar syrup (see page 75)

50g (1¾oz) white modelling chocolate (Cocoform)

EQUIPMENT

Basic equipment (see pages 8–11)

Sheet of paper

Savoy piping nozzle 1.5cm (⅝") round

Metal skewer

Daisy cutters (PME)

MAKES 25-30 FINGER ÉCLAIRS

1 Draw two parallel lines on a piece of paper that are 8cm (3⅛") apart: this will be the template for the éclairs. Place onto a baking tray and secure a sheet of baking paper over the top using dots of the mixture in the corners.

2 Fit a plastic piping bag with a 1.5cm (⅝") plain piping nozzle and fill with the choux pastry mixture. Pipe sausages of the mixture between the lines on the template so they are all approximately the same length. Remove the template before baking.

3 Brush egg wash over the éclairs with a pastry brush, then score straight lines along the top of them with a fork.

4 Bake the éclairs at 200°C/400°F/gas mark 6 for 10–12 minutes first. Once the éclairs have puffed up, turn down the oven to 180°C/350°F/gas mark 4 and continue baking for five to 10 minutes. Do not open the oven door whilst the pastry is baking.

5 Once the éclairs are golden brown, turn down the oven

to 150°C/300°F/gas mark 2 and bake for another five to 10 minutes to dry them out.

6 Take one éclair out of the oven at this stage and gently press it. If it is hard, take all of the éclairs out of the oven and allow to cool on a wire rack. If the pastry is still soft, leave them in the oven at the lower temperature to dry out for another five minutes before checking again.

7 Make two holes in the back of each éclair with a metal skewer in preparation for the filling.

8 Place the coffee-flavoured crème pâtissière in a plastic piping bag, then cut off the tip with a pair of scissors to make a tiny hole. Fill each of the choux buns with a small amount of crème pâtissière through the pre-made holes. To keep the filling fresh, make sure you place the buns in the fridge until you are ready to move onto the next step.

9 Spoon approximately 50g (1¾oz) of fondant icing into a small bowl and put to one side for the daisy centres. Place the remaining fondant icing in a large, heat-resistant bowl and add a couple of tablespoons of sugar syrup. Heat the icing gradually in a microwave until it is approximately 37°C (body temperature). If the fondant isn't soft enough to dip the buns into, add more sugar syrup. Do not over-heat the icing or it will lose its shine.

10 Add a few drops of coffee extract to the icing and stir it through to make it pale brown in colour. Hold the éclair upside down, dip the top into the icing and remove any excess on the edge of the bowl. Leave to dry icing-side-up on a tray.

11 Repeat to decorate the remaining éclairs with the icing. To keep the filling fresh, make sure you only work with a small amount of éclairs at a time and return them to the fridge once you are finished with them.

12 Roll out 50g (1¾oz) of white modelling chocolate into a thin sheet and cut out several flowers of different sizes using the daisy cutters. Place each flower on your palm and make a dent in the centre with a ball tool.

13 Melt the fondant icing you set aside earlier, place it in a piping bag and pipe a little dot in the centre of each flower. Arrange the daisies on the éclairs and secure with some melted fondant icing.

TOP TIP

You can make the daisy decorations in advance and store them in an airtight container for a few days until you are ready to use them.

PARISIAN POOCH ÉCLAIRS

EDIBLES

6 x coffee éclairs (see pages 122–123)

Sugarpaste: 10g (¼oz) blue, 15g (½oz) brown, 10g (¼oz) red, 10g (¼oz) white

Small amount of chocolate, melted

EQUIPMENT

Basic equipment (see pages 8–11)

MAKES 6 PARISIAN POOCH ÉCLAIRS

1 Make the coffee éclairs up to step 11 (see page 123). Roll out 10g (¼oz) of white and 10g (¼oz) of blue sugarpaste into 3cm x 6cm (1⅛" x 2⅜") rectangles that are approximately 5mm (¼") thick. Place the blue rectangle on top of the white one and cut in half. Place one half of the paste on top of the other piece and cut in half again. Repeat once more to create a blue and white-striped block. Slice it carefully into six equal pieces with a sharp knife. Trim the sides of each piece and place them on the centre of the éclairs.

2 Make 12 x 1cm (⅜") diameter balls from 15g (½oz) of brown sugarpaste. Roll them into teardrop shapes and flatten them gently to make the dogs' ears. Make six

5mm (¼") diameter balls from the brown paste then roll them into little sausages for the tails.

3 Roll six tiny balls of red sugarpaste and put them to one side. Divide the remaining red paste into six equal pieces and roll them into balls. Flatten down each ball and secure a tiny ball in the centre of each one.

4 Melt a small amount of chocolate, place it in a paper piping bag and cut a tiny hole in the end of the bag. Use the chocolate to attach the hat, ears, tail and shirt to each éclair. Pipe faces on the end of the éclairs with the melted chocolate.

COLOURFUL CROQUEMBOUCHE

EDIBLES

Choux buns

1½ x choux pastry recipe (see page 110)

1½ x crème pâtissière recipe (see page 112)

2kg (4lb 6½oz) pack of fondant icing mix (made up according to the packet instructions)

Liquid food colours: blue, green, orange, pink, purple, yellow

Sugar syrup (see page 75)

Egg wash (egg yolks)

Caramel

600g (1lb 5¼oz) caster sugar

60g (2oz) glucose syrup

240ml (8½fl oz) water

Decoration

200g (7oz) white modelling chocolate (Cocoform)

EQUIPMENT

Basic equipment (see pages 8–11)

40cm high x 18cm diameter (16" x 7") cone-shaped dummy (or see the top tip on page 132 to make a paper cone)

Savoy piping nozzle: 8mm (5/16") round

Metal skewer

Heat-resistant kitchen gloves (recommended)

Rose leaf cutter (FMM)

Rose leaf veiner

CHOUX BUNS

1 Draw a series of 3cm (1⅛") diameter circles on a piece of paper to make a template, spacing them a few centimetres apart. Place onto a baking tray and secure a sheet of baking paper over the top using dots of the mixture in the corners.

2 Fit a plastic piping bag with an 8mm (5/16") plain round piping nozzle and fill with the choux pastry mixture.

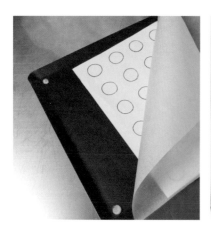

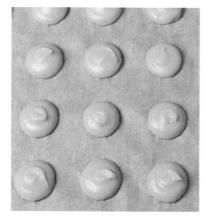

Squeeze the bag and pipe 3cm (1⅛")
diameter circles onto the baking paper,
keeping them as even as possible. You will
need approximately 180–195 small choux
buns. Remove the template before baking.

3 Brush egg wash over the circles with a
pastry brush then press the top with a fork
to make pretty, round choux buns.

4 Bake the buns at 220°C/425°F/gas
mark 7 for 15 minutes. Once the pastry
has puffed up, turn down the oven to
180°C/350°F/gas mark 4 and continue
baking for five to 10 minutes. Do not open
the oven door whilst the pastry is baking.

5 Once the choux buns are golden
brown, turn the oven down to
150°C/300°F/gas mark 2 and bake for
another five to 10 minutes to dry them out.

6 Take one choux bun out of the oven at
this stage and gently press it. If it is hard,
take all of the buns out of the oven and
allow to cool on a wire rack. If the pastry is
still soft, leave them in the oven at a lower
temperature to dry out for another five to
10 minutes before checking again.

7 Make a hole in the bottom of each
choux bun with a skewer in preparation
for the filling.

8 Place the crème pâtissière in a plastic
piping bag, then cut off the tip with a pair
of scissors to make a tiny hole. Fill each
of the choux buns with a small amount of
crème pâtissière through the pre-made
hole. To keep the filling fresh, make sure
you place the buns in the fridge until you
are ready to move onto the next step.

9 Place 300g (10½oz) of the made-up
fondant icing in a large, heat-resistant
bowl then add a couple of tablespoons
of sugar syrup. Heat the icing gradually in

a microwave until it is approximately 37°C (or body temperature). If it isn't soft enough to dip the choux buns into, add more sugar syrup. Do not overheat the icing or it will lose its shine.

10 Divide the total amount of choux buns into six groups. Add a small amount of pink liquid food colour to the fondant icing to make it pale pink. Dip the first group of buns one by one into the pale pink icing and remove any excess on the edge of the bowl. Leave them to dry icing-side-up on a tray.

11 Repeat steps 9–10 to decorate the remaining buns in different colours of fondant icing.

TOP TIPS

To make your icing go further, colour any leftover pale pink icing with purple food colour to make the icing a darker colour. You can also do this with any leftover yellow icing to make green and orange.

To keep the filling fresh, make sure you only work with a small number of buns at a time and return them to the fridge once you have iced them.

MAKING THE CROQUEMBOUCHE

12 At this stage you will need a 40cm high x 18cm diameter (16" x 7") cone: you can either buy a cone-shaped polystyrene dummy or make a paper cone following the instructions in the tip below. Place on a cake stand or display board.

TOP TIP

To make a paper cone, take a 40cm (16") square of paper (the length of the paper = the height of the cone), draw an arc from corner to corner on the diagonal and cut along the line. Using the top corner as the tip of the cone, bring one side of the paper to meet the other. Adjust the sides so that the diameter of the base is at least 6cm (2³/₈") smaller than the cake stand or board you are using. Secure with some sticky tape. Repeat with a large sheet of silicone baking paper and place this cone over the top of the paper cone, securing with a little caramel (see left) as tape won't stick to the silicone paper (you can do this once you've made the caramel).

13 Before you start making the caramel, make sure that all the choux buns are filled and divided into groups of the same colour. Weigh 600g (1lb 5¼oz) of caster sugar into a bowl and add 60g (2oz) of glucose on top (this way the glucose won't stick to the bowl). Place 240ml (8½fl oz) of water into a pan then pour the sugar and glucose onto it. This method allows the sugar to dissolve without needing to stir it, preventing any crystallisation on the utensils.

14 Bring to a medium heat slowly. Do not stir as this will cause the sugar to crystallise. Use a clean pastry brush and hot water to clean the caramel from the sides of the pan: try not to add too much extra water when doing so.

15 As the caramel starts to turn light brown, quickly remove it from the heat and dip the bottom of the pan in a sink of cold water or place on a cool, damp cloth to stop it cooking further. If you have a digital thermometer, the temperature of the caramel should be approximately 165°C before you remove it from the heat or else it won't be strong enough to hold the buns in place.

TOP TIP

As I wanted to use a pastel colour scheme for the croquembouche, I have only heated the caramel to light brown stage. For a traditional croquembouche, heat the caramel for a little longer until it turns golden brown.

16 Cut a piece of baking parchment to the same size as the cake stand or board, then sit the cone on the paper. Dip the back and base of a choux bun into the caramel and stick it to the bottom of the cone: I recommend you wear heatproof gloves to protect yourself from the hot caramel. Repeat with the remaining choux buns, working around the cone in layers and arranging the colours evenly. Try not to put two choux buns of the same colour next to one another. Make sure all the buns are secure and leave to set completely. Remove the cone and place the croquembouche on a cake stand or board.

17 Roll out some white modelling chocolate into a thin sheet, then cut out several leaves with a rose leaf cutter. Vein each leaf in a rose leaf veiner. Pinch the bottom of the leaves with your fingers to give them shape then attach them around the tower with a little caramel to fill in any gaps.

Chocolate is sometimes seen as a complex medium to work with, as you often need to temper the chocolate in order to get good results. In this chapter, I have provided some easy methods for tempering, as well as a range of different chocolate treats that look delicious but are simple to make. I always recommend using high-quality couverture chocolate for all of these projects if you want a superior taste and a professional finish.

CHOCOLATE

TREATS

HOW TO TEMPER CHOCOLATE

Tempering is crucial in most chocolate work if you want to achieve a finished product that looks shiny, sets hard and snaps crisply when broken. If chocolate is not tempered properly, the texture becomes brittle and white spots may appear as a result of fat bloom. You can buy chocolate that doesn't need tempering, but it is low-quality and contains other fats instead of cocoa butter. There are several different ways you can temper chocolate but I have provided two of the simplest methods that you can easily achieve in your kitchen at home.

METHOD 1: TEMPERING BY ADDING CHOCOLATE

EDIBLES

1kg (2lb 3½oz) white, milk or dark high-quality couverture chocolate

EQUIPMENT

Basic equipment (see pages 8–11)

Large metal bowl

Large saucepan for bain-marie (optional)

These are the temperature guidelines I use when tempering:

	Melting temperature (A)	Cooling temperature (B)	Ready-to-use temperature (C)
Dark	48–55°C	28–29°C	30°C
Milk	45–50°C	27–28°C	29°C
White	40–45°C	26°C	28°C

1 Chop up all the chocolate finely using a large, sharp knife. Place ⅔ of the chocolate in a large metal bowl.

2 Half-fill a saucepan with hot water and place the bowl over it, making sure the bowl doesn't touch the water. Slowly heat the water, ensuring it doesn't boil. Stir the chocolate regularly using a flexible spatula so that the chocolate melts evenly.

3 Once the chocolate has melted, check the temperature with a digital thermometer. When the chocolate reaches

the correct melting temperature (see table, A), remove the bowl from the heat and add the final ⅓ of the chopped chocolate, stirring continuously. The chocolate

TOP TIP

Alternatively, place the chocolate in a heat-resistant bowl and microwave on a low heat in 30-second bursts, stirring between each burst to prevent the chocolate from burning.

should drop to the appropriate cooling temperature (see table, B). If it is too hot, stir the chocolate to bring the temperature down.

4 Return the bowl to the bain-marie for a few seconds to raise the temperature very slightly and melt the remaining chocolate. When the chocolate reaches the ready-to-use temperature (see table, C), remove from the heat.

5 To test the chocolate, place a small amount on a piece of greaseproof paper and leave it to cool. If the chocolate sets hard and looks shiny then the chocolate has been tempered correctly. If the chocolate does not set or has a dull finish, then repeat the same method to heat, cool and reheat it to the temperatures given in the table.

TOP TIP

If you want to temper less than a kilo of chocolate, it will be more difficult to maintain its temperature. To help overcome this, use a smaller bowl to minimise the surface area of the chocolate.

METHOD 2: TEMPERING USING ICED WATER

EDIBLES

1kg (2lb 3¼oz) white, milk or dark high-quality couverture chocolate

EQUIPMENT

Basic equipment (see pages 8–11)

Microwaveable bowl (optional)

Large metal bowl and large saucepan for bain-marie (optional)

Bowl filled with iced water

1 Heat all of the chocolate over a bain-marie or in a microwave following steps 1–2 of Method 1. Make sure you stir the chocolate regularly to prevent it from burning.

2 Once the chocolate has melted, check the temperature with a digital thermometer. When the chocolate reaches the correct melting temperature (see table, A), remove it from the heat and place the bowl of chocolate in a bowl of iced water. Do not let any water get into the bowl or the chocolate will seize. The chocolate at the bottom of the bowl should set immediately, then after a few seconds remove the bowl from the iced water and stir well. Repeat until it cools to the correct temperature (see table, B).

3 Return the bowl to the bain-marie and allow the bottom of the bowl to warm up for a few seconds, or heat in the microwave for a few seconds at a time, carefully bringing the chocolate to the temperature when it is ready to use (see table, C).

4 Test the chocolate following step 5 in Method 1.

EARL GREY TEA 'NAMA CHOCO' GANACHE

INGREDIENTS

350ml (12¼fl oz) whipping cream
(containing 35% milk fat)

30g (1oz) loose Earl Grey tea leaves

45g (1½oz) glucose syrup

400g (14oz) dark chocolate (containing
70% cocoa solids), chopped

30g (1oz) butter

2–3 tbsp pure cocoa powder

EQUIPMENT

Basic equipment (see pages 8–11)

Hand blender

30.5cm x 15cm (12" x 6") shallow
container, e.g. baking dish

Presentation box

MAKES 27 X 3CM (1⅛") GANACHE CUBES

1 Line a shallow container with cling film.

2 Pour 320ml (11¼fl oz) of the whipping cream into a saucepan with the Earl Grey tea leaves and place over a medium-low heat, leaving 30ml (1fl oz) of the cream to one side. Remove the pan from the heat just before the mixture reaches boiling point. Leave the cream to infuse for an hour then pass through a sieve.

3 Weigh the infused cream and add extra cream to make it up to 320ml (11¼fl oz) again, if necessary. Place in a pan over a low heat, add the glucose syrup and allow to dissolve.

4 When the glucose syrup has dissolved, place the chocolate in a bowl and pour the cream and glucose mixture over the chocolate. Leave the chocolate to melt for a few minutes then mix the cream through it. At first it will look as if it has split but continue to mix the ganache with a hand blender to emulsify it. Try not to add too much air to the mixture.

5 Once you have achieved a smooth and creamy texture, pour the mixture into the container and leave to set in the fridge.

6 Choose a presentation box for the chocolates then cut the ganache to the same size as the box. Slice through the ganache to make smaller, individual portions, then sprinkle cocoa powder over the top before serving in the box.

TOP TIP

If you want to add extra flavours to this recipe, such as cinnamon or chilli, simply add them with the tea leaves and allow to infuse.

You can also make mouth-watering chocolate truffles from this recipe. Simply use your hands or a melon baller to make small balls from the set ganache, dip them in melted chocolate and roll in cocoa powder for a classic finish.

CHOCOLATE NEST CUPCAKES

INGREDIENTS

Cupcakes

80g (2¾oz) salted butter

150g (5¼oz) plain flour

250g (8¾oz) caster sugar

50g (1¾oz) pure cocoa powder

1tbsp baking powder

200ml (7fl oz) full-fat milk

2 large eggs

DECORATION

100ml (3½fl oz) whipping cream

500g (1lb 1¾oz) chocolate ganache or chocolate-flavoured buttercream (see pages 92–93 or 76)

200g (7oz) tempered dark chocolate (see pages 136–137)

60 small chocolate eggs

EQUIPMENT

Basic equipment (see pages 8–11)

Small marble slab

Large chocolate scraper

Melon baller (optional)

MAKES 12 CUPCAKES

1 Place a marble slab in the freezer to chill for at least 30 minutes.

2 Bake the cupcakes following the recipe on page 74, using the ingredients above. Add the cocoa powder with the dry ingredients. Once they have cooled, scoop out the centre of each cupcake with a melon baller or spoon.

3 Pour the cream into the bowl of an electric mixer then whip it with the whisk attachment until it starts to form soft peaks (see page 76). Continue to whisk the cream by hand until the cream forms firm peaks.

4 Place a tablespoon of whipped cream into the hole in each of the cupcakes.

5 Make up some chocolate ganache and place it in a plastic piping bag. Pipe some chocolate ganache in the centre of each cupcake, then spread it over the top with a palette knife.

6 Remove the marble slab from the freezer. Place some tempered chocolate in a paper piping bag and cut off the very tip. Pipe several fine lines of chocolate back and forth over the marble slab.

7 As soon as you have finished piping, lift the chocolate off the marble using a large scraper. Fold the chocolate into a ring with your hands to make a birds' nest and place on top of a cupcake. Pipe and scrape more chocolate in the same way to build up each nest.

8 To finish, place several chocolate eggs in the centre of each nest.

TOP TIP

I filled the cupcakes with whipped cream as it complements the sweetness of the chocolate cupcakes. For different flavour combinations, you could try using praline or caramel as an alternative filling.

VERY BERRY CHOCOLATES

INGREDIENTS

Chocolate feuilletine biscuits

80g (2¾oz) milk chocolate

25g (just over ¾oz) hazelnut praline (or peanut butter)

100g (3½oz) SK Petit Crunch (Pailleté Feuilletine)

Mixed berry chocolate mousse

180g (6¼oz) frozen mixed berries

35g (1¼oz) caster sugar

2.7g leaf gelatine, soaked in cold water

130g (4½oz) milk chocolate, chopped

220ml (7¾fl oz) whipped cream (containing 35% milk fat)

Chocolate glaze

75ml (2½fl oz) double cream

30g (1oz) glucose syrup

120ml (4¼fl oz) water

120g (4¼fl oz) caster sugar

60g (2oz) pure cocoa powder

6g leaf gelatine, soaked in cold water

DECORATION

Royal iced pansies (see page 188)

EQUIPMENT

Basic equipment (see pages 8–11)

4cm (1½") round cutter

Small half-sphere silicone baking mould: 5cm (2")

Digital thermometer

MAKES 25 MOUSSE-FILLED CHOCOLATES

CHOCOLATE FEUILLETINE BISCUITS

1 Melt the milk chocolate and praline together. Fold in the Petit Crunch.

2 Pour the mixture onto a sheet of greaseproof paper, place another sheet on top then roll it out thinly using a rolling pin. Leave to set in the fridge.

3 Once the mixture is firm, cut out 25 circles with a 4cm (1½") round cutter. If you don't have enough space to cut out all the circles, melt the remaining mix and re-use it in the same way as before.

MIXED BERRY CHOCOLATE MOUSSE

4 Place the frozen mixed berries and caster sugar together in a pan. Heat gently until the berries have defrosted and the sugar has dissolved. Blitz the mix with a handheld blender.

5 Add the pre-soaked gelatine and pass the mixture through a fine sieve.

6 Place the chocolate in a bowl and pour the hot berry mix over the chocolate. Mix well as the chocolate melts and allow to cool to approximately 45°C.

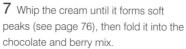

7 Whip the cream until it forms soft peaks (see page 76), then fold it into the chocolate and berry mix.

8 Transfer the mousse to a large plastic piping bag and pipe it to the top of each well in the half-sphere mould. Place a feuilletine biscuit on top of the mousse in each half-sphere. Leave to set in the fridge for approximately an hour, or the freezer for 10 minutes.

CHOCOLATE GLAZE

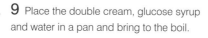

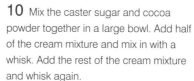

9 Place the double cream, glucose syrup and water in a pan and bring to the boil.

10 Mix the caster sugar and cocoa powder together in a large bowl. Add half of the cream mixture and mix in with a whisk. Add the rest of the cream mixture and whisk again.

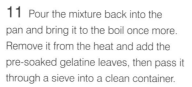

11 Pour the mixture back into the pan and bring it to the boil once more. Remove it from the heat and add the pre-soaked gelatine leaves, then pass it through a sieve into a clean container.

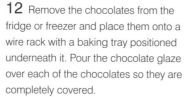

12 Remove the chocolates from the fridge or freezer and place them onto a wire rack with a baking tray positioned underneath it. Pour the chocolate glaze over each of the chocolates so they are completely covered.

13 To serve, place the chocolates on a plate and decorate with royal iced pansies (see page 188).

TOP TIP

The glaze can be stored for three to four days if you don't want to use it immediately.

TIRAMISU CANDLES

INGREDIENTS

Sponge discs

30g (1oz) egg yolks and 45g (1½oz) egg whites
(approx. 1 medium egg, separated)

45g (1½oz) caster sugar

45g (1½oz) plain flour, sieved

Chocolate tubes

250g (8¾oz) tempered white chocolate
(see pages 136–137)

Sabayon

4 egg yolks

100g (3½oz) caster sugar

½ vanilla pod

100ml (3½fl oz) coffee liqueur (e.g. Kahlúa)

500g (1lb 1¾oz) mascarpone

Assembly

80ml (2¾fl oz) espresso coffee

80g (2¾oz) pale yellow sugarpaste or marzipan

Black food colour pen (SK)

Dust food colours: orange, red

EQUIPMENT

Basic equipment (see pages 8–11)

30cm (12") square baking tray

Round cutters: 4cm (1½") for small candles, 6cm (2⅜") for
large candles

3.5cm and 5.5cm (1⅜" and 2¼") diameter cylindrical
formers, e.g. cardboard tubes

Acetate sheets: 2 x 15cm x 22cm (6" x 8½") for large
candles, 4 x 15cm x 11cm (6" x 4¼") for small candles
and an A4 sheet for discs

Medium-sized metal bowl and saucepan for bain-marie

Marble slab

Sticky tape

6 squares of greaseproof paper

Metal skewer (optional)

MAKES TWO LARGE (15CM HIGH X 6CM DIAMETER/6" X 2⅜") AND FOUR SMALL
(11CM HIGH X 4CM DIAMETER/4" X 1½") CHOCOLATE CANDLES

SPONGE DISCS

1 Follow the recipe for sponge fingers on pages 98–101, using the ingredients for sponge discs above. Instead of piping the mixture, pour it onto a square baking tray and spread it out evenly. Bake the sponge sheet for approximately 10–12 minutes, then leave to cool.

2 Cut out 12 discs from the sponge sheet with a 6cm (2⅜") round cutter for the large candles. Cut out 24 discs with a 4cm (1⅛") round cutter for the small candles.

CHOCOLATE CYLINDERS AND DISCS

3 Wrap the formers in cling film and temper the white chocolate (see pages 136–137).

4 Place an acetate sheet of the correct size on a marble slab. Spread some of the chocolate evenly over the sheet using a small, cranked palette knife: the chocolate will need to be 2mm ($^1/_{16}$") deep for a large candle and slightly thinner for the smaller candles. Lift the sheet off the slab with a chocolate scraper and leave until the surface has firmed slightly.

5 Use a chocolate scraper to remove approximately 1.5cm ($^5/_8$") of chocolate from one end of the sheet. Place a prepared cylinder at one end of the sheet. Wrap the sheet loosely around the former so the chocolate doesn't stick to it. Overlap the end of the sheet without chocolate and secure with a little tape. Repeat to make the remaining chocolate cylinders.

6 Cover an A4 sheet of acetate with chocolate in the same way, then use a round cutter to cut out four 6cm ($2^3/_8$") discs for the large candles and eight 4cm ($1^1/_2$") discs for the smaller candles. Leave to set.

SABAYON

7 Whisk the egg yolks, caster sugar and the seeds from ½ a vanilla pod together in a medium-sized metal bowl. Add the coffee liqueur to the mixture.

8 Place the bowl over a bain-marie and keep whisking the mixture until it is thick and creamy. Remove the mixture from the heat and leave it to cool down in some iced water or place in the fridge.

9 Put the mascarpone in the bowl of a stand mixer and whisk until soft and creamy. Add the cooled sabayon to the bowl a little at a time and continue to whisk until it reaches soft-peak consistency.

TOP TIP

Mixing the sabayon with mascarpone to make a thicker cream will prevent the filling from leaking out of the candles and give it a richer flavour.

ASSEMBLY

10 Unwrap the acetate sheet from around a large chocolate cylinder and stand the cylinder upright on a square of greaseproof paper.

11 Place a white chocolate disc in the bottom of the tube, then place two sponge discs on top of it. Put the sabayon mixture into a large plastic piping bag, then pipe a layer of the mixture on top of the sponge. Place another sponge disc on top, then use a teaspoon or pastry brush to splash a little coffee onto it. Do not soak the bottom layer of sponge with coffee or it may leak.

12 Insert two more layers of sponge, another layer of sabayon and the final sponge layer. Top it with a final layer of sabayon, level it with a palette knife and finish with a chocolate disc. Fill the smaller cylinders in the same way. Leave to set in the fridge for a couple of hours.

13 Place the melted white chocolate in a piping bag and cut a small hole in the end. Pipe some chocolate around the top of the cylinders to make it look like the candle is melting.

14 For the large candles, roll approximately 20g (¾oz) of pale yellow sugarpaste or marzipan into a ball. Model it into a teardrop shape then pinch the end to make it into a flame. For small candles, you only need 10g (¼oz) of sugarpaste or marzipan per candle.

15 Colour a cocktail stick with a black food colour pen and insert it into the bottom of the flame. Dust $^2/_3$ from the top of the flame with orange dust food colour, then dust $^1/_3$ from the top with red dust food colour.

16 Carefully make a tiny hole in the centre of the top chocolate disc with a scribing tool or metal skewer. Insert the flame decoration into the hole.

MINT CHOCOLATE CHARLOTTES

INGREDIENTS

Chocolate sponge fingers

3 medium eggs, separated

90g (3oz) caster sugar

¼ vanilla pod

30g (1oz) pure cocoa powder

60g (2oz) plain flour, sieved

30ml (1fl oz) sugar syrup

Mint chocolate mousse

45g (1½oz) egg yolks (approx. 2½ medium eggs)

40g (1½oz) caster sugar

200ml (7fl oz) full-fat milk

Bunch of fresh mint leaves, chopped (approx. 20g/¾oz)

3.5g (⅛oz) leaf gelatine, soaked in iced water

35g (1¼oz) dark chocolate, chopped

150ml (5¼fl oz) double cream

⅕ x chocolate glaze recipe (see page 142)

EQUIPMENT

Basic equipment (see pages 8–11)

2–3 large baking trays

6 x 5.5cm diameter x 3.5cm high (2¼" x 1⅜") dessert rings

6 x 10cm (4") squares of baking paper

1cm (⅜") round piping nozzle

Digital thermometer (optional)

A large bowl of iced water

Decorative ribbon in a colour of your choice

MAKES 6 INDIVIDUAL DESSERTS

CHOCOLATE SPONGE FINGERS

1 Preheat the oven to 170°C/340°F/gas mark 3½.

2 Use a dessert ring to draw six 5.5cm (2¼") diameter circles on a sheet of baking paper, leaving 2–3cm (¾–1⅛") between them, then turn it upside down and place on a baking tray. Line two to three large baking trays with baking paper. Fit a large plastic piping bag with a 1cm (⅜") piping nozzle.

3 Follow the method for making sponge fingers on pages 98–101, using the ingredients listed above. Add the cocoa powder to the mixture at the same time as the flour.

4 Use a swirling motion to pipe six circles within the templates, then pipe 50 sponge fingers that are approximately 9cm (3½") long.

5 Bake for 10–12 minutes until the sponge starts to colour. Remove from the oven and leave to cool on a wire rack.

6 Use a dessert ring to trim the circles of sponge to size again. Place each of the dessert rings on a square of baking paper, then place a sponge disc into the bottom of each ring. Brush each sponge ring with plenty of sugar syrup to make sure they are not too dry.

7 Cut the sponge fingers in half then trim to approximately 4cm (1½") in length.

MINT CHOCOLATE MOUSSE

8 Whisk the egg yolks and caster sugar together until pale and thick.

9 Blitz the milk and chopped mint together with a hand blender, then place in a pan and slowly bring to the boil. If you don't have a hand blender, chop the mint very finely.

10 Pour half of the hot milk onto the egg mixture, whisking continuously to prevent the eggs from scrambling. Add the rest of the milk.

11 Return the mixture to the pan and stir over a low heat until it coats the back of a spatula. Do not allow it to boil. If you have a digital thermometer, heat the mixture to approximately 80°C.

12 Squeeze the water out of the pre-soaked gelatine, add to the pan and mix in well.

13 Place the chocolate in a bowl and pour the mixture through a sieve onto the chocolate. Leave the bowl to cool down in some iced water.

14 Whilst the mixture is cooling down, whip the double cream into soft peaks (see page 76).

15 Fold half of the whipped cream into the cold chocolate mixture. Add the rest of whipped cream and fold it through.

16 Divide the mixture evenly between the six prepared dessert rings. Leave to set in the fridge.

ASSEMBLY

17 Once they are ready to serve, run a warm knife around each ring to help you remove the mousse.

18 Attach the sponge fingers around the mousses, then spoon some of the chocolate glaze over the top of each one.

19 To finish, tie a ribbon around each of the desserts to help hold the sponge biscuits in place.

For an extra-special touch, top each dessert with a flake of edible gold leaf.

LISA'S GIFT CAKES

INGREDIENTS

Almond chocolate sponge

65g (2¼oz) egg whites (approx. 2 large egg whites)

15g (½oz) caster sugar

60g (2oz) ground almonds

10g (¼oz) pure cocoa powder

45g (1½oz) icing sugar

Chocolate mousse

25g (just over ¾oz) caster sugar

25ml (just over ¾fl oz) water

30g (1oz) egg yolks (approx. 1½ large egg yolks)

80g (2¾oz) dark chocolate (60% cocoa solids), chopped

200ml (7fl oz) whipping cream

Caramel mousse

80g (2¾oz) caster sugar

320ml (11¼fl oz) double cream

80ml (2¾fl oz) full-fat milk

80g (2¾oz) egg yolks (approx. 4 large egg yolks)

50g (1¾oz) hazelnuts, chopped

3.5g (⅛oz) leaf gelatine, soaked in iced water

DECORATION

500g (1lb 1¾oz) tempered white chocolate (see pages 136–137)

EQUIPMENT

Basic equipment (see pages 8–11)

18cm (7") square baking tray

18cm (7") square cake tin

Large metal bowl and saucepan for bain-marie

Bowl of iced water (optional)

1 or 2 small marble slabs, chilled in a freezer

18cm x 10cm (7" x 4") rectangle of greaseproof paper

MAKES 16 MINI CAKES

ALMOND CHOCOLATE SPONGE

1 Preheat the oven to 190°C/375°F/gas mark 5. Line a square baking tray with baking paper.

2 Whisk the egg whites until they form soft peaks, then add the caster sugar and continue to whisk until the mixture forms stiff peaks.

3 Sieve the ground almonds and cocoa powder together, then fold them into the mixture a little at a time.

4 Pour the mixture onto the baking tray, spread it out evenly and sprinkle with icing sugar. Bake for 15 minutes, then leave to cool on a wire rack.

5 Line an 18cm (7") square cake tin with greaseproof paper or cling film. Place the pre-baked sponge sheet in the bottom of the lined tin.

CHOCOLATE MOUSSE

6 Whisk the caster sugar, egg yolks and water together in a bowl then place the mixture into a bain-marie. Continue to whisk until thick and creamy then mix in the chocolate. Pour the mixture into a bowl and cool it down in a bowl of ice water or leave in the fridge.

7 Whisk the whipping cream to soft-peak consistency (see page 76) and fold it through the mixture. Pour the mixture over the sponge sheet and spread it out evenly. Leave to set in the fridge for an hour or the freezer for 10 minutes.

CARAMEL MOUSSE

8 Heat the caster sugar in a large saucepan and allow it to dissolve to make caramel, swirling the pan as it melts to prevent it from burning.

9 Meanwhile, place the cream and milk in a different saucepan and bring to the boil.

10 Once the caramel is ready, keep the pan on a high heat and add ⅓ of the cream mixture little by little to prevent the caramel overflowing.

11 Add the egg yolks to the mixture and whisk. Turn the heat down low and stir continuously until it is thick enough to coat the back of a spatula, then remove from the heat. If you have a digital thermometer, it should be approximately 70–85°C in temperature.

12 Squeeze out the pre-soaked gelatine leaves, then add to the mixture along with the chopped hazelnuts. Leave it to cool down in a bowl of iced water until thickened.

13 Pour the mixture over the previous layer of chocolate mousse and leave to set in the fridge for an hour or the freezer for 30 minutes.

ASSEMBLY

14 Once the mousse has set, remove the sheet from the tin and cut it into 16 x 4cm (1½") cubed mini cakes.

15 Temper the white chocolate (see pages 136–137).

TOP TIP

You will only need 400–500g of chocolate to cover 16 mini cakes (approximately 25g/just over ¾oz per cake), but you need to use more to maintain the temperature of the chocolate once it has been tempered.

16 Place a small amount of melted chocolate in the centre of a chilled marble slab. Spread it out thinly with a large, cranked palette knife. Slide a chocolate scraper under the thin layer of chocolate to lift it off the slab. The chocolate will need to be flexible: as the marble slab will still be very cold, the first layer of chocolate may have cooled down too quickly and is likely to be too stiff to wrap around the cakes, so discard the first layer.

17 Repeat step 16 but use the edge of the scraper to cut the chocolate into an 18cm x 10cm (7" x 4") rectangle, using the paper template as a guide. Lift the chocolate off the marble with the scraper and check its flexibility. Place one of the mini cakes at the edge of the

rectangle, leaving enough chocolate at one end to go around the cake. Wrap the chocolate around the cake, then stand it up. Gather and twist the chocolate at the top while the chocolate is still pliable.

18 Place the cakes on a tray and leave in the fridge to defrost completely before serving.

When I was working as a pastry chef, I often made these little cake parcels to serve at afternoon tea. They used to call these gift cakes 'Elise', but I have named them after the head chef, Lisa Crowe, as a thank you for all that she taught me.

STRAWBERRY MOUSSE POTS

INGREDIENTS

Biscuit moelleux au chocolat

105g (3¾oz) dark chocolate, chopped

55g (2oz) butter

50g (1¾oz) egg yolks (approx. 2½ large egg yolks)

100g (3½oz) egg whites (approx. 2½ large egg whites)

55g (2oz) caster sugar

18g (½oz) plain flour, sieved

Sugar syrup (optional, see page 75)

Strawberry mousse

160g (5½oz) fresh strawberries

40g (1½oz) sugar

6g (just under ¼oz) gelatine, soaked in iced water

180ml (6¼fl oz) double cream

40g (1½oz) strawberry jam (optional)

DECORATION

120ml (4¼fl oz) double cream

1tsp icing sugar, to taste

10 SK Transfer Sheets for Chocolate: Pink Roses

100g (3½oz) tempered white chocolate
(see pages 136–137)

1–2tbsp piping gel (SK)

A sheet of rice paper

EQUIPMENT

Basic equipment (see pages 8–11)

15cm x 30cm (6" x 11½") baking tray, lined

10 x 5.5cm diameter x 3.5cm high (2¼" x 1⅜")
dessert rings

Large bowl of iced water

Hand blender

Butterfly craft punch

MAKES 10 STRAWBERRY MOUSSE POTS

BISCUIT MOELLEUX AU CHOCOLAT

1 Preheat the oven to 190°C/375°F/gas mark 5. Line a baking tray with greaseproof paper.

2 Melt the chocolate and butter together in a pan. Add the egg yolks and whisk through.

3 Place the egg whites in a bowl of an electric mixer fitted with a whisk attachment. Whisk them until they form soft peaks, then add the caster sugar and continue to whisk to make a glossy, stiff-peak meringue.

4 Mix ⅓ of the meringue into the melted chocolate and whisk through. Add another ⅓ of the meringue and fold through with a spatula. Add the remaining ⅓ of the meringue with the sieved flour and fold through.

5 Pour the batter over a baking tray and bake for 10–12 minutes. It is baked when the top of the cake springs back gently to the touch or a skewer inserted into the centre comes out clean. Remove once baked and leave to cool on a wire rack.

6 Use a dessert ring to cut out 10 circles from the sponge sheet. Place a sponge circle in the base of each dessert ring and leave on a lined baking tray.

STRAWBERRY MOUSSE

7 Place the fresh strawberries and sugar in a bowl and use a hand blender to blitz them into a strawberry purée.

8 Place half of the purée in a pan and heat it gently. When the purée is warm, squeeze out any excess water from the pre-soaked gelatine, add to the pan and mix in well. Once the gelatine has dissolved, return the heated mixture to the other half of the purée and leave to cool down and thicken.

9 Whilst the strawberry mixture is cooling down, whip the double cream until it forms soft peaks (see page 76). Add the cream to the strawberry mixture a little at a time.

10 Brush some sugar syrup over the sponge layers if desired.

11 Pipe or spoon the mousse mixture evenly into each dessert ring, filling to just below the rim. Place a teaspoon of strawberry jam in the centre if desired. Leave to set in the freezer for one to two hours.

WHITE CHOCOLATE DECORATION

12 Once the surface has set, whip another 120ml (4¼fl oz) of double cream to soft-peak consistency, adding a teaspoon of icing sugar to taste (see page 76). Spread evenly over the top of each ring with a small palette knife. Leave to set in the fridge for another one to two hours.

13 To help you remove the mousse from the rings, run a

TOP TIP

Try adding some chopped and roasted walnuts, almonds or hazelnuts to the mousse to add crunch.

warm, small sharp knife around the inside of each ring. If it is still difficult to remove the mousse, place in the freezer for five to 10 minutes and try again.

14 Cut 10 transfer sheets to approximately 20cm x 4cm (8" x 1½") in size, so they are slightly longer than the circumference and taller than the height of a dessert ring. Wrap a sheet around a dessert ring and measure the length of the overlap, which should be approximately 2.5cm (1").

15 Temper the white chocolate (see pages 136–137). Place the transfer sheet on a board with the cocoa butter pattern facing upwards and spread a thin layer of chocolate over it, making sure to cover it completely. Scrape off the chocolate from the 2.5cm (1") overlap. Leave until the surface of the chocolate has dried slightly and has changed from glossy to matt.

16 Lift the acetate sheet and wrap it around one of the mousses with the chocolate design facing inwards. Overlap the ends and apply a little pressure so the chocolate sticks together. Leave to set in the fridge for approximately 30 minutes to an hour.

17 Repeat steps 15–16 for the nine remaining mousses.

18 Peel back the acetate sheet from around each mousse just before serving. If the join opens slightly, stick it back down with a touch of melted chocolate.

19 Spread a very thin layer of piping gel over the top of the mousse to achieve a shiny finish. If it is not easy to spread, warm the gel up slightly in a microwave or add a little clear alcohol, e.g. gin or vodka.

20 To finish, cut butterfly shapes from a sheet of rice paper using a craft punch. Fold them in half to make the wings stand up and secure to the mousse pots with a little melted chocolate.

MINI EASTER EGGS

INGREDIENTS

Chocolate shells

300g (10½oz) tempered white chocolate
(see pages 136–137)

Sponge cake trimmings

Coconut jelly

200ml (7fl oz) coconut milk

80g (2¾oz) caster sugar

250ml (8¾fl oz) full-fat milk

8g (¼oz) leaf gelatine, soaked in iced water

1 ripe mango

EQUIPMENT

Basic equipment (see pages 8–11)

3 x 5cm (2") plain half-sphere or half-egg
chocolate moulds

Lint-free cloth

Hand blender

MAKES 12 FILLED CHOCOLATE EGGS

CHOCOLATE SHELLS

1 Polish the inside of the chocolate moulds with a lint-free cloth or kitchen paper. Line two to three baking trays with greaseproof paper.

2 Pour some tempered chocolate into each mould, fill it almost to the top and swirl it around until the chocolate has completely coated the mould. Tap the mould lightly to eliminate any air bubbles. After a few seconds, turn the mould upside down over a large bowl and let the excess chocolate run out so you are left with a thin layer. Pull a chocolate scraper across the surface of the mould to clean it. Leave the mould flat-side-down on the lined tray and allow the chocolate to set for a few hours.

3 Repeat step 2 using the remaining moulds to make 24 chocolate shells.

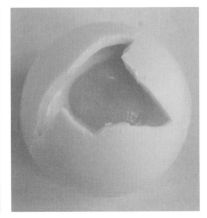

4 Once set, carefully remove the half-spheres from the moulds whilst warming a baking tray in the oven on a low heat. Place the flat sides of the half-spheres on the tray to soften the chocolate slightly then stick two halves together. Run your finger around the seam to neaten the join. Repeat to make 12 chocolate spheres and leave to set.

5 Heat the blade of a sharp knife in a bowl of hot water and use it to make a jagged hole in the top of each shell.

6 Carefully place small pieces of sponge cake in the bottom of the eggs.

TOP TIP

This is a great way to make use of the trimmings from a sponge cake.

COCONUT JELLY

7 Place the coconut milk, sugar and full-fat milk in a pan and bring to the boil.

8 Squeeze out any excess water from the pre-soaked gelatine and add to the pan. Remove from the heat and leave to cool down completely.

9 Spoon the jelly into each egg shell and leave them to set in the fridge.

10 Chop the mango into small pieces and blend to make a purée. Drop a teaspoonful of mango purée on top of the coconut jelly to make the yolk.

CHOCOROONS

INGREDIENTS

35g (1¼oz) ground almonds

40g (1½oz) icing sugar

5g (just under ¼oz) pure cocoa powder

35g (1¼oz) egg whites (approx. ¾ of a large egg white)

30g (1oz) caster sugar

Liquid food colour of your choice

100g (3½oz) filling of your choice, e.g. buttercream (approx. 3g (⅛oz) per macaroon)

300g (10½oz) tempered dark chocolate (70% cocoa solids) (see pages 136–137)

Transfer sheets for chocolate in your chosen design

EQUIPMENT

Basic equipment (see pages 8–11)

Savoy piping nozzle: 7–8mm (¼– ⅜") round

Template (see page 203)

Chocolate dipping fork

The sweetness of the macaroons with the bitterness of the dark chocolate makes a delicious combination and it doesn't matter if your macaroons don't come out looking perfect as the chocolate coating will hide any flaws.

MAKES 32 x 3.5CM (1⅜") DIAMETER MACAROONS

1 Preheat the oven to 160°C/325°F/gas mark 3.

2 Line a large baking tray with baking paper, then slide the template underneath the lining.

3 Sieve the ground almonds, icing sugar and cocoa powder together or place them in a food processor and blitz them into a fine powder.

> ### TOP TIP
>
> If you choose to sieve them, make sure to discard any large almond pieces and top up with more ground almonds to maintain the correct amount.

4 Place the egg whites in the bowl of a stand mixer fitted with a whisk attachment and whisk until they form soft peaks. Gradually add ⅓ of the caster sugar to the egg whites, whisking continuously. Add the remaining sugar little by little and whisk until it forms glossy, stiff peaks. Add a few drops of your chosen food colour at this stage.

5 Fold half of the dry ingredients into the meringue mixture with a spatula and mix well. Add the rest of the dry ingredients and mix again until it reaches a smooth and shiny consistency. When you lift the mixture with a spatula, it should fall off in a ribbon-like trail but the mixture should still stay in peaks. Try not to mix it too much at this stage.

6 Fit a large piping bag with a 7–8mm (¼–⅜") round piping nozzle and fill the bag with the mixture. Pipe 64 small rounds 2mm (¹⁄₁₆") inside the macaroon templates. A small peak will have formed on the top of each macaroon: tap the bottom of the tray with your hand until the peaks disappear. Leave at room temperature for approximately 30 minutes until the surface has dried slightly. The macaroons are ready to bake once they are no longer sticky to the touch.

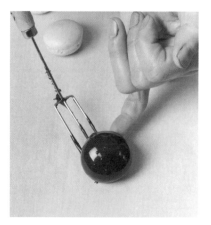

7 Bake in a preheated oven for two minutes, then turn the oven down to 120°C/250°F/gas mark ½ and bake for 15 minutes. The macaroons should have risen slightly and have a smooth surface. Remove from the oven and leave to cool down.

TOP TIP

The secret to making good macaroons is all in the baking: every oven is slightly different so try baking a few trial macaroons first to become familiar with your own oven's settings.

8 Once cool, sandwich the macaroon halves together with your chosen filling.

9 Temper some dark chocolate (see pages 136–137). Spread the chocolate onto a chocolate transfer sheet in your chosen design (see page 163) and cut it into small strips that are approximately 3.5cm long and 1cm wide (1⅛" x ⅜").

10 Pick up the macaroons one at a time on a chocolate dipping fork, then dip them into the tempered chocolate so that they are completely covered before placing on a sheet of greaseproof paper. Lay a strip of the chocolate-covered transfer sheet over the top of each macaroon, then carefully peel off the acetate backing. Leave to set completely.

Whatever the occasion, flowers always make beautiful decorations for cakes, pastries and desserts. Over the next few pages, I will explain how to pipe a selection of popular flowers using royal icing, buttercream or meringue, as well as using edible flowers for decoration. Many of the piping techniques are transferable so you can create the same flower with different icings.

USING
FLOWERS
FOR DECORATION

MERINGUE FLOWERS

Italian meringue is the best type of meringue for piping flowers, as the addition of boiled sugar syrup makes it more stable than traditional recipes. I use meringue to pipe simple flowers that you can pop on ice creams, cakes and desserts to add decoration and texture. You will need to bake the meringue flowers once they are piped as per the recipe.

ITALIAN MERINGUE

INGREDIENTS

Sugar syrup

140g (5oz) caster sugar

30ml (1fl oz) water

Meringue

70g (2½oz) egg whites (approx. 1¾ large egg whites)

20g (¾oz) caster sugar (or vanilla sugar)

Seeds from ¼ vanilla pod, or a few drops of vanilla essence (if not using vanilla sugar)

Liquid food colour of your choice (optional)

EQUIPMENT

Basic equipment (see pages 8–11)

Digital thermometer

MAKES ENOUGH FOR 20 ROSES OR
20 FIVE-PETAL FLOWERS

1 Preheat the oven to 90–100°C/190–200°F/gas mark low.

2 Place the egg whites into the bowl of an electric mixer, making sure the bowl is clean and grease-free before you start.

3 Make the sugar syrup following the instructions on page 75. As you are boiling the sugar syrup, whisk the whites on a high speed until they form soft peaks.

4 Turn down the speed on the mixer and add 20g (¾oz) of sugar to the egg whites. Continue to whisk until the mixture forms stiff peaks. Measure the temperature of the sugar syrup: if it hasn't reached 115°C at this point, turn down the mixer even further.

5 As soon as the syrup reaches 118–120°C, put the mixer on a slow speed and slowly pour the syrup into the egg white mixture.

6 Turn the mixer back up to a high speed. Once the meringue mix has risen up nicely, set the mixer to a medium speed and continue to mix until it has cooled to room temperature. Add the vanilla pod seeds or essence and a few drops of liquid food colour as required.

MERINGUE ROSE

YOU WILL NEED...

1 x Italian meringue recipe (see page 173)

2 large plastic piping bags

Large petal piping nozzle: no. 121 (Wilton)

20 x 5–7.5cm (2–3") squares of waxed paper

Icing nail

MAKES 20 MERINGUE ROSES

1 Preheat the oven to 100°C/200°F/gas mark low.

2 Fit one of the piping bags with a no. 121 piping nozzle and place some of the meringue mixture in the bag. Place a small amount in the second bag and cut approximately 1cm (³/₈") off the tip.

TOP TIP

Do not put too much mix in the piping bag or it will be difficult to handle and you'll squeeze the air out of the meringue.

3 Stick a square of greaseproof paper to the top of an icing nail with a little of the meringue. Pipe a small cone in the centre of the paper using the bag without a nozzle.

4 Change to the piping bag fitted with a nozzle and hold it so the wider part of the nozzle is at the bottom and the narrower end at the top. Start piping at the very top of the cone and turn the nail anticlockwise (or clockwise if you are left-handed), piping slowly all the way around the centre to make a rose bud.

5 Starting from the join, pipe the first petal a third of the way around the bud. Start piping the second petal from where the first petal meets the bud, so they are overlapping. Pipe a third petal in the same way so it overlaps the second petal.

6 Pipe five more petals around the previous petals in the same way.

7 Lift the waxed paper off the icing nail with the flower on top and place on a baking tray. Repeat to make approximately 20 flowers from the meringue then bake for two hours until the outside is crisp. Leave to cool down completely before using as decoration.

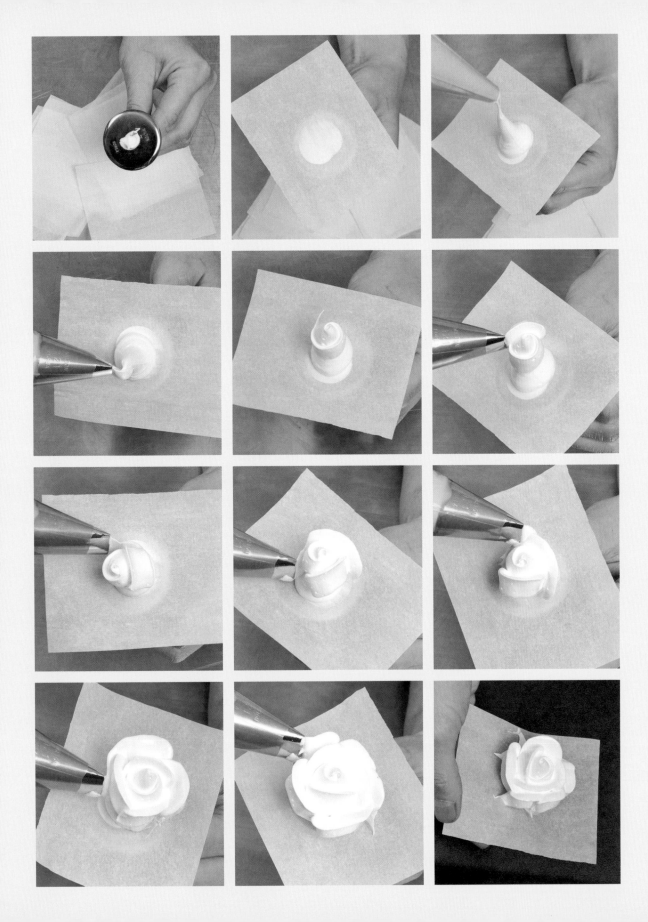

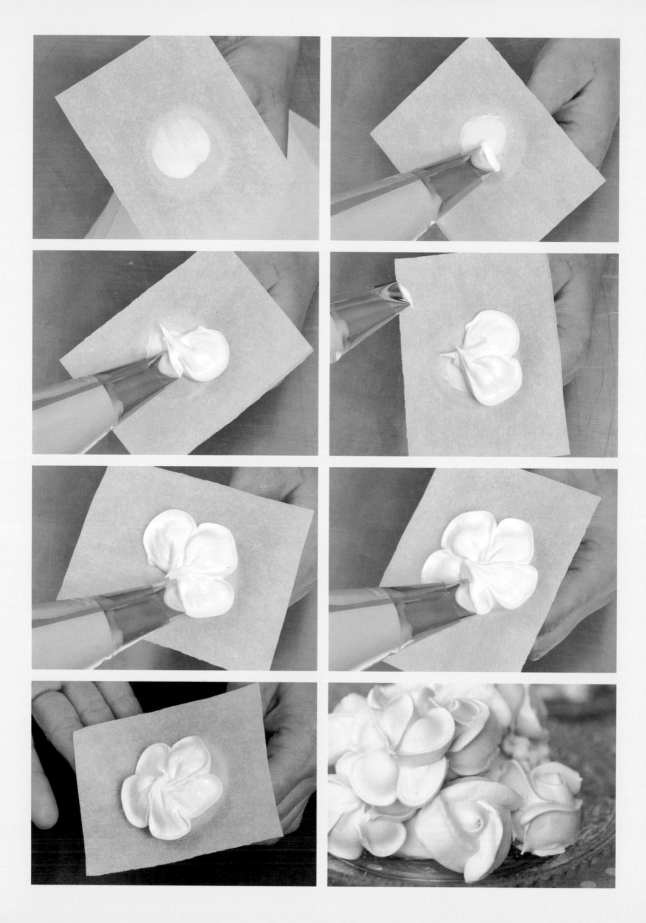

MERINGUE FIVE-PETAL FLOWER

YOU WILL NEED...

1 x Italian meringue recipe (see page 173)

Large plastic piping bag

Large petal piping nozzle: no. 104 (Wilton)

20 x 5–7.5cm (2–3") squares of waxed paper

Icing nail

MAKES 20 MERINGUE FIVE-PETAL FLOWERS

1 Preheat the oven to 100°C/200°F/gas mark low.

2 Fit a plastic piping bag with a no. 104 piping nozzle and place some of the meringue mixture in the bag. Attach a square of waxed paper to the top of an icing nail with a little meringue.

3 Hold the piping nozzle at a 40° angle to the centre of the paper, with the wider part at the bottom and the narrower end at the top. Pipe the first petal diagonally towards the corner of the waxed paper, turning the nail anticlockwise as you pipe (or clockwise if you are left-handed). Bring the petal back into the centre to finish it.

4 Place the piping nozzle just below the first petal and pipe a second petal the same size and shape next to the first.

5 Pipe three more petals in the same way, making sure the last petal finishes alongside the first.

6 Lift the waxed paper off the icing nail with the flower on top and place on a baking tray. Bake the flowers for two hours until the outside is crisp. Leave to cool down completely before using as decoration.

TOP TIP

To make sure the petals are even, draw five dividing lines on the paper before you start to make five equal sections. Use the sections as a guide when piping each of the petals.

BUTTERCREAM FLOWERS

Buttercream flowers are a popular choice as they can be piped directly onto a cake or cupcake and have a soft texture that is easy to eat. You can use the buttercream recipe of your choice (see page 76) but it should have a stiff consistency so the flower will hold its shape. If you are colouring the buttercream, I recommend using liquid food colours for a pastel tone and paste food colours if you want a stronger shade.

BUTTERCREAM ROSETTE

YOU WILL NEED…

1 x basic buttercream recipe (see page 76)
Large plastic piping bag
Large open star nozzle: 1M (JEM)
12 cupcakes (see page 74)

MAKES 12 BUTTERCREAM ROSETTES

1 Fit a piping bag with a large open star nozzle and place some of the buttercream into the bag.

2 Hold a cupcake in one hand and position the piping bag perpendicular to the top of the cake.

3 Starting in the centre of the cupcake, pipe outwards in a circular motion towards the edge of the cake. Release the pressure to finish.

LARGE BUTTERCREAM ROSE

YOU WILL NEED…

1 x basic buttercream recipe (see page 76)

2 large plastic piping bags

Large coupler/adapter nozzle (optional)

Savoy piping nozzle: 7mm ($^5/_{16}$") round

Large petal piping nozzle: no. 121 (Wilton)

15cm x 2cm (6" x $^3/_4$") strip of greaseproof paper

12 cupcakes (see page 74)

MAKES 12 LARGE BUTTERCREAM ROSES

1 Fit a piping bag with a large coupler nozzle and attach a 7mm ($^5/_{16}$") round piping nozzle to it. If you don't have a coupler nozzle, fit one piping bag with a 7mm ($^5/_{16}$") nozzle and a second with a no. 121 nozzle.

2 Place some of the buttercream into the bag fitted with a round nozzle and pipe 12 large cones on a strip of greaseproof paper. Leave the centres to firm in the fridge for an hour or in the freezer for 10 minutes.

3 Once firm, level the tops of the cupcakes and place a rose centre in the middle of each one.

4 Change the nozzle in the coupler to a no. 121 piping nozzle (or prepare a second piping bag). Pipe petals around the rose centre following steps 4–5 for Meringue Roses on page 174, turning the cupcake anticlockwise (or clockwise if you are left-handed) as you pipe. Add another three layers of petals around the rose to cover the top of the cupcake.

MINI BUTTERCREAM ROSES WITH LEAVES

YOU WILL NEED...

1 x basic buttercream recipe (see page 76)

Liquid food colours: green and another colour of your choice

Leaf nozzle (optional)

Large coupler/adapter nozzle (optional)

Savoy piping nozzle: 7mm ($^5/_{16}$") round

Large petal piping nozzle: no. 121 (Wilton)

36 x 5cm (2") squares of greaseproof paper

12 cupcakes (see page 74)

MAKES 36 MINI BUTTERCREAM ROSES WITH LEAVES

1 Colour 3tbsp of buttercream with a touch of green liquid food colour. Place the green buttercream into a large paper piping bag and cut a V-shape into the tip (or fit the bag with a leaf nozzle) and put to one side. Colour the rest of the buttercream with the liquid food colour of your choice.

2 Fit a piping bag with a large coupler nozzle and attach a 7mm ($^5/_{16}$") round piping nozzle to it. If you don't have a coupler nozzle, fit one piping bag with a 7mm ($^5/_{16}$") nozzle and a second with a no. 121 nozzle. Place some more buttercream into the bag fitted with a 7mm ($^5/_{16}$") nozzle. Pipe three cone shapes that are approximately 1cm x 1cm ($^3/_8$" x $^3/_8$") in size on each piece of greaseproof paper to make the rose centres.

3 Change the nozzle in the coupler to a no. 121 piping nozzle (or prepare a second piping bag) and fill with buttercream. Pipe three layers of petals around each of the centres, following steps 4–5 for the Meringue Roses.

4 Place all the roses on a tray and leave to set in the fridge for an hour, or leave in the freezer for 10 minutes. Once they have firmed up, remove the paper from underneath the roses and arrange three roses on top of each cupcake. Use soft buttercream as glue if necessary.

5 Use the green buttercream to pipe a leaf between each rose, following the steps on page 192.

BUTTERCREAM HYDRANGEA

YOU WILL NEED...

1 x basic buttercream recipe (see page 76)

Leaf nozzle (optional)

Liquid food colours: green and another colour of your choice

Large plastic piping bag

Petal piping nozzle: no. 58R (if you are right-handed) or 58L (if you are left-handed)

150 x 5cm (2") squares of waxed paper

12 cupcakes (see page 74)

MAKES APPROX. 108 HYDRANGEAS WITH LEAVES

1 Colour 3tbsp of buttercream with green liquid food colour for the leaves. Place the green buttercream into a large paper piping bag and cut a V-shape into the tip (or fit the bag with a leaf nozzle) and put to one side.

2 Colour the remaining buttercream with the liquid food colour of your choice. Fit a large plastic piping bag with a no. 58 piping nozzle and fill the bag with the buttercream.

3 Pipe one four-petal flower onto each square of paper following steps 3–5 on page 177 for Meringue Five-Petal Flowers. You need approximately 12 four-petal flowers to cover the top of one cupcake. Leave to set in the fridge for

an hour, or the freezer for 10 minutes.

4 Spread any leftover buttercream thinly over the surface of the cupcake. Remove the square of paper from the bottom of one flower and place it in the centre of the cake, then position five to six flowers around the edge. Place three to four flowers on top of the first layer to hide any gaps.

5 Use the green buttercream to pipe leaves around the flowers, following the steps on page 192.

BUTTERCREAM CHRYSANTHEMUM

YOU WILL NEED...

1 x basic buttercream recipe (see page 76)

Liquid food colours of your choice

Large paper piping bag

Chrysanthemum piping nozzle: no. 81 (Wilton)

12 cupcakes (see page 74)

MAKES 12 BUTTERCREAM CHRYSANTHEMUMS

1 Fit a large paper piping bag with a no. 81 piping nozzle. Colour the buttercream with the liquid colour of your choice, spread a thin layer onto each cupcake and place the remaining buttercream in the bag.

2 Hold the bag so that the piping nozzle looks like a U-shape or a 'smile' and position the tip of the nozzle 1cm (3/8") out from the centre of the cupcake. Start piping a 1.5cm (5/8") line to the edge of the cupcake and pull away gently at the end to create a slightly pointed petal.

Continue piping petals around the top of the cupcake in the same way until you come back to the first.

3 Pipe a second layer of petals starting 5mm (1/4") inside the first layer that sit in between the previous petals.

4 Pipe the third, fourth and fifth layers of petals in the same way, starting 5mm (1/4") inside the previous layer each time. For the sixth and final layer, pipe slightly shorter petals in the centre of the cupcake.

ROYAL ICING FLOWERS

Royal icing can be used with very small piping nozzles to create
more detailed flowers that will dry firm and hold their shape.
These handy little flowers are great for popping on biscuits,
cupcakes and chocolates and can be piped in advance and
stored ready for use.

ROYAL ICED FOUR-PETAL FLOWERS

YOU WILL NEED...

Stiff-peak royal icing (see page 17)
Liquid food colours: yellow and another colour of your choice
Small paper piping bag
Piping nozzles: no. 57 (PME)
Small squares of waxed paper, slightly bigger than the size of flower you want to create

1 Attach a square of waxed paper to the top of an icing nail using a small amount of royal icing. Colour some of the royal icing with a little liquid food colour of your choice.

2 Fit a small paper piping bag with a no. 57 petal nozzle and place a couple of teaspoons of stiff-peak royal icing into the bag.

3 Holding the piping bag between your index finger and thumb, tilt the nozzle at a slight angle so that the wider end is touching the centre of the waxed paper.

4 Pipe the first petal diagonally towards the corner of the waxed paper, turning the nail 90° anticlockwise as you pipe (or clockwise if you are left-handed). Bring the petal back into the centre to finish it. Pipe slightly smaller petals if you wish to make a five-petal flower.

5 Colour a small amount of icing with a little yellow liquid food colour. Place a little yellow icing in a piping bag, snip off the tip and pipe a tiny dot in the centre of the flower.

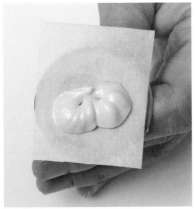

ROYAL ICED PANSIES

YOU WILL NEED...

Stiff-peak royal icing (see page 17)
Liquid food colours: black, yellow and two more colours of your choice
2 small paper piping bags
Large paper piping bag
Piping nozzle: no. 58
Small squares of waxed paper, slightly bigger than the size of flower you want to create

1 Divide the icing between two bowls and colour with different liquid food colours. Place ½tbsp of one colour in a paper piping bag, then place 2tbsp of the second colour in another paper piping bag. Cut the tips off the bags of icing.

2 Fit a large piping bag with a no. 58 petal nozzle. Use the first bag of coloured icing to pipe a line down the same side of the larger bag as the curved part of the nozzle. Pipe down the other side of the bag with the second colour of icing to create a two-tone effect.

3 Attach a square of waxed paper to the top of an icing nail using a small amount of icing.

4 Hold the bag so the nozzle is at a slight angle with

the wider part of the nozzle touching the centre of the paper. Pipe the first petal following step 4 for Royal Icing Four-Petal Flowers (see page 187).

5 Pipe another petal next to the first petal, then pipe two more petals on top of the first two to create a double layer.

6 For the last petal, turn the icing nail anticlockwise (or clockwise if you're left-handed) while you pipe a full-size petal. Leave to dry overnight.

7 To finish, paint a few fine lines over the petals with a small paintbrush and some black liquid food colour. Pipe a small dot of yellow icing in the centre (see step 5 for Royal Icing Four-Petal Flowers).

TOP TIP

If you find that the consistency of the royal icing is too soft once you've added liquid food colours, add a little more icing sugar to make it firmer.

ROYAL ICED ROSES

YOU WILL NEED...

Stiff-peak royal icing (see page 17)
Liquid food colours: yellow and two more colours of your choice
2 small paper piping bags
Piping nozzle: no. 58
Squares of waxed paper

1 Attach a square of waxed paper to the top of an icing nail using a small amount of icing.

2 Fit a piping bag with a no. 58 nozzle and place a couple of tablespoons of stiff-peak royal icing in the bag. Place some more icing in another paper piping bag without a nozzle. Cut the tip off the bag and pipe a small cone in the centre of the nail.

TOP TIP

If you're not confident at piping, you may find it easier to pipe around a firm central cone. You can either make a cone out of sugarpaste or pipe some royal icing cones in advance and leave them to firm up.

3 Hold the nozzle perpendicular to the icing nail with the wider part of the nozzle at the bottom and the narrower end at the top. Turning the nail anticlockwise (or clockwise if you are left-handed), pipe continuously around the top of the cone for one-and-a-half turns.

4 Turning the nail in the same direction, pipe three petals around the bud, overlapping the edges of the petals slightly.

5 Pipe five more petals around the previous layer in the same way.

FIVE-PETAL FLOWERS

YOU WILL NEED...

Soft-peak royal icing (see page 17)
Small paper piping bag

1 Place a couple of tablespoons of soft-peak icing in a piping bag then cut off the tip of the bag. Pipe a small dot, then release the pressure from the bag and pull the icing downwards to create a teardrop shape.

2 Pipe two more teardrop shapes diagonally around the central point, either side of the first. Pipe two more petals on the opposite side and pipe a dot in the centre to finish.

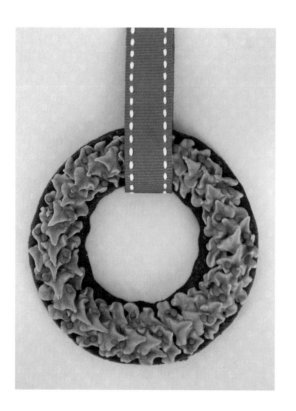

LEAVES

YOU WILL NEED...

Stiff-peak royal icing (see page 17)
Liquid food colour: green
2 paper piping bags
Medium leaf piping nozzle: no. ST51 (PME) (optional)

1 Colour some stiff-peak royal icing with green liquid food colour. Fit a paper piping bag with an ST51 nozzle or simply cut the tip of the bag into a small V-shape.

2 Hold the bag at a 45° angle and place the nozzle on the surface. Squeeze out a small amount of icing and move the bag back and forth quickly a few times to create a wavy leaf. Lift the bag and pull it away gently to create a pointed tip.

EDIBLE FLOWERS

Edible flowers are an easy way to add a decorative touch to a cake, pastry or dessert. Popular edible flowers include roses, nasturtiums, borage, calendulas, pansies and violets. Simply sprinkle the blooms over sweets and desserts to add colour, flavour and texture.

1 Make sure to buy edible flowers from a specialist vendor – I used Maddock's Farm Organics. Do not eat flowers purchased from garden centres, nurseries, supermarkets, florists, or flowers collected from parks, etc. Most of these flowers will have been treated with pesticides and herbicides that can be toxic if eaten.

2 Always check before eating any flowers to ensure they are completely edible as some are poisonous if eaten.

3 On rare occasions, some people have proved to be allergic to edible flowers, particularly in the case of people with strong pollen allergies. Always check with your guests before serving.

Create a unique table centrepiece at a wedding or afternoon tea by coordinating the piped flowers on a dessert or cake with the floral theme. Ask your florist for flowers which are non-toxic and ensure they don't come into contact with any edible part of the dessert or cake.

TEMPLATES

Dressing Table Biscuits,
pages 51–56

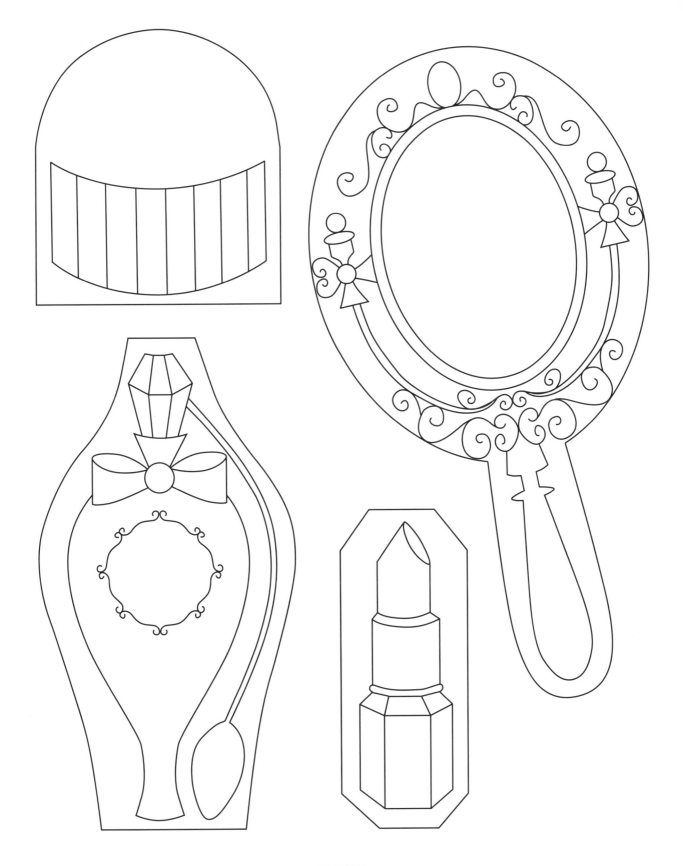

Patterned Swiss Rolls, pages 86–91

Checked pattern

Cherry pattern

Apple pattern

Patterned Opera Cakes, pages 94–97

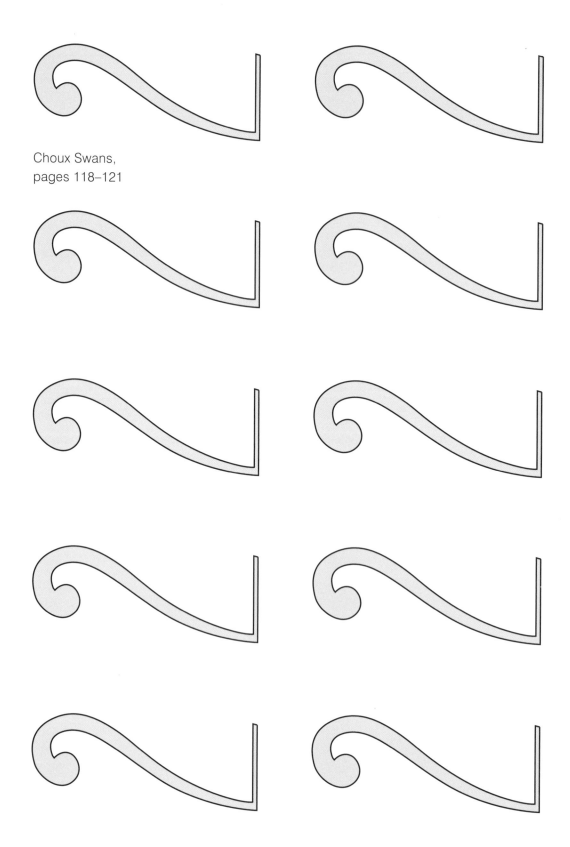

Choux Swans,
pages 118–121

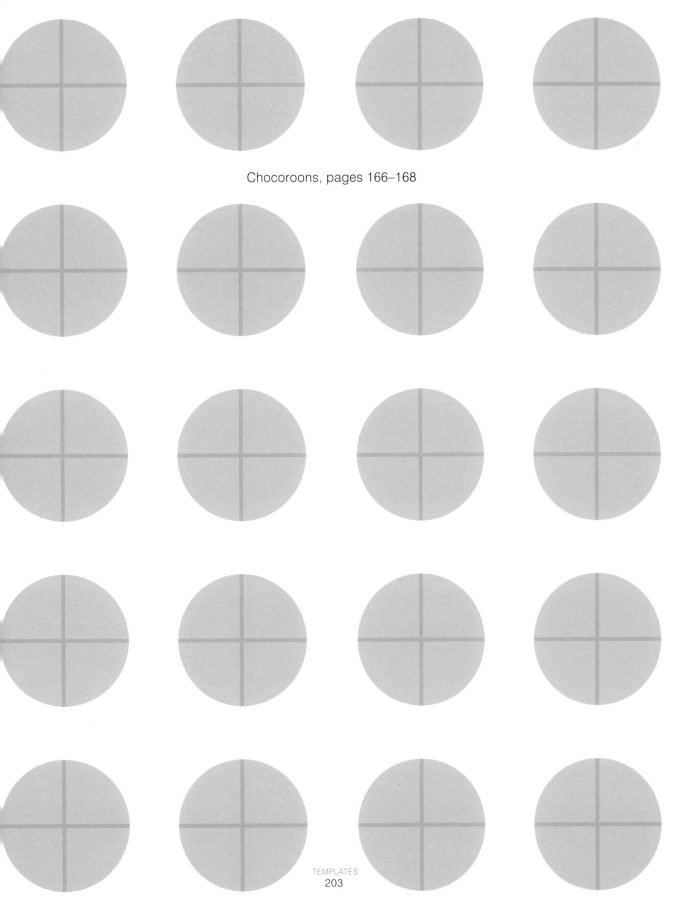

Chocoroons, pages 166–168

INDEX

RECIPES

TECHNIQUES

OTHER BOOKS BY MAKIKO SEARLE

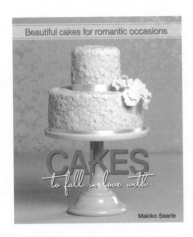

CAKES TO FALL IN LOVE WITH

(B. Dutton Publishing, 2011)

You can't help but fall head over heels with this irresistible collection of contemporary cakes for romantic occasions. If you're celebrating a wedding, anniversary, engagement, Valentine's Day or simply being in love, you can make your very own gorgeous cakes to make every celebration extra special.

From adorable miniature cakes for an engagement party to the most luxurious of wedding cakes, cake makers of all abilities can follow Makiko's step-by-step instructions to make beautiful cakes in their own kitchen. A wide choice of cake recipes, icings and fillings are given, along with basic techniques and plenty of tips if you're new to cake decorating.

Each of the 12 cake projects is beautifully photographed and comes complete with easy-to-follow instructions, a full list of edibles and equipment, and step-by-step pictures. Designs include jewel-encrusted mini cakes, a pretty basket brimming with summer blooms, a wonderfully opulent ten-tier wedding cake covered in pristine white peonies, and Maki's signature Temari ball cakes for a truly contemporary twist.

THE ART OF SUGARCRAFT
BY SQUIRES KITCHEN TUTORS

(B. Dutton Publishing, 2014)

The Art of Sugarcraft is the only book of its kind to present a vast range of skills, techniques, projects and expert advice from 20 of the world's leading cake decorating tutors. Ideal for keen cake makers, budding bakers and sugarcraft hobbyists of all abilities, it takes the reader through everything from basic recipes to masterclasses in sugarcraft, with everything in between.

This beautifully presented, fully illustrated book is divided into six chapters for ease of use: Baking and Patisserie; Chocolate; Foundation Sugarcraft; Extended Sugarcraft; Masterclasses; and Commercial Cake Decorating. Each section offers a broad range of traditional techniques, new skills and contemporary ideas – all with step-by-step instructions and photography – as well as projects to create at home, including special-occasion cakes and irresistible treats.

Each tutor offers a wealth of knowledge and individual style and all are leading names at Squires Kitchen, the oldest and one of the most popular schools of its kind in the UK. As one of the contributing tutors, Makiko presents an elegant white chocolate croquembouche tower adorned with rice paper peonies and a colourful summer wedding cake showcasing the pâte décor technique.

SUPPLIERS

Squires Kitchen, UK
3 Waverley Lane
Farnham
Surrey
GU9 8BB
0845 61 71 810
+44 (0) 1252 260 260
www.squires-shop.com

Squires Kitchen
International School, UK
The Grange
Hones Yard
Farnham
Surrey
GU9 8BB
0845 61 71 810
+44 (0) 1252 260 260
www.squires-school.co.uk

Distributors

UK

Culpitt Ltd.
Northumberland
www.culpitt.com

Guy, Paul & Co. Ltd.
Buckinghamshire
www.guypaul.co.uk

Squires Kitchen
Surrey
www.squires-shop.com

For your nearest sugarcraft
supplier, please contact your
local distributor.

Europe

Cake Supplies
Netherlands
www.cakesupplies.nl

Dom Konditera LLC
Belarus/Russia
www.domkonditera.com

Sugar World – Aliprantis Ltd.
Greece
www.sugarworld.gr

Tårtdecor
Sweden
www.tartdecor.se

 B. Dutton Publishing is an award-winning publisher of cake
decorating titles. To find out more about our books, follow us at
www.facebook.com/bduttonpublishing.